What People Are Saying About
David Stern and *Are You For Real?!*

"I have been privileged to know David Stern for almost fifteen years and have watched him make changes and challenge himself to get to this exciting point in his life and career. I am proud to be his colleague and friend. David is a truly extraordinary coach, trainer, manager, and sales professional who has honed and shared his many skills, helping individuals and corporations to really succeed. He is authentic, engaging, motivating, ethical, and always interesting—as is his new book—a wonderful read!"

— Belinda Plutz, President, Career Mentors Inc.

"Is this author for real? In my forty-five-year business career, I learned that the one key factor of successful people is that they always put the people they work or deal with, up front and center. For them, the customer, colleagues, and the job always come first and then the rewards—including money—follow. When you read *Are You For Real?!*, you will find this theme woven into every paragraph. I have called David Stern a friend for nearly forty-five years. He is always honest, straightforward, and devoted to doing what is good for others first, and then he thinks about himself. I am proud to say, 'David Stern is for REAL.'"

— Hershel Jacobowitz, S.E.V.P. B&H Photo

"I have had the privilege of knowing David Stern for the past seven years. He is an amazing colleague and friend, and it is about time he shared his experiences with the world. He is one of the best salespeople I have ever met. Thank you, David, for writing this book."

— Kristen Esposito, Vice President,
Macy's Tourism Marketing

"I have known David Stern since 1993 when he helped me launch a new industry called pre-paid phone cards for World Telecom, Inc., and he became the #1 sales executive in the country. Few people in my career have had such a profound and positive impact on my life as David. His shining skills, deep sense of purpose, hard work, and tenacity make him who he is today—a true success story! I highly recommend that anyone in sales, or considering it for a career, read his book. He loves helping people, and if this planet had more David Sterns, everyone would be a lot better because of it!"

— Kevin M. Young, President, Young
Private Consulting, LLC, Kirkland, WA

"After reading this book, I'm ready to say, 'Get ready for the new me.' If David can get real, so can I."

— John Christopher Bryant, Founder of
www.BryantWealthManagement.com

"*Are You For Real?!* is a powerful read that takes you on one man's journey to the top while teaching you his secrets to success along the way. Both compelling and practical, this book gives you exactly what you need: a swift kick in the butt and an I-can-do-it attitude. I'd buy anything Stern was selling!"

— Jennifer Powers, Author of *Oh, Shift! How to Change Your Life with One Little Letter*

"Over the years we have observed David in action as an exhibitor in our USA Pavilions at trade shows all over the world: he is always on the move, always observing, always innovative, always full of new ideas and suggestions. Never satisfied with half-measures."

— Björn Bieneck, President & CEO,
B-FOR International

"David's narrative is compelling and the pace never drops. *Are You For Real?!* is a must-read for young sales professionals while experienced hands will enjoy the familiar. Reading this book, you will understand what qualifies Stern to be a sales coach."

— Ramjee Chandran, Writer and
Publisher-Editor, Explocity Group

"David was very clear in helping me understand that when in sales, I would be building better, stronger, and longer relationships with my customers."

— Anna Ligia, Author of *The Omnia Project*

"The time management and database management skills discussed in this book are nothing that I haven't heard before, *but* the way David explains them makes me want to focus on them."

— Adrianne Carlino Gentile, Author of
Integrity in the Mirror

"Ha! This book got me. Now I know that all the excuses I have been making for myself will no longer work if I want to climb the ladder to success."

— Jeff Barnes, Author of *The Wisdom of Walt: Leadership Lessons from the Happiest Place on Earth*

"David is the real deal! He has evolved to become one of the best sales and personal coaches in the country today. His knowledge and proven expertise didn't come from attending Wharton or the Harvard Business School. Instead, he listened to one of our fellow mentors, who said, "If you want to really know how to be successful, don't listen to anybody who hasn't already achieved it. If they knew how, they'd already be successful." David became a graduate student of that philosophy. He not only learned the 'how-to's', but he learned the reasons 'why.' I believe every great teacher must always start out as a great student. That is what you get with Coach Stern, so take full advantage of that!"

— Tom Carroll, P.A., CRS, ABR, Owner of Assist-2-Sell, Sell and Buy Realty

"I love the puzzle analogy David discusses, I feel it will help me stay better focused on my goals."

— Renee Gillard, Author of *No More Insulin*

"Reading *Are You For Real?!* got me thinking and planning for positive change."

— Brent Scarpo, Author of *The Red Balloon*

"After reading David's message in this book, I will no longer feel down when a prospect says NO to me."

— Grace Fiorre, Author of *The Nothing Spirit*

"*Are You For Real?!* is very real! It's a sometimes humorous yet serious self-examination that underscores the importance of those 'basics' that less experienced salespeople need to develop and seasoned sales professionals strive to maintain throughout their careers. Thank you, David Stern, for sharing these valuable pearls."

— Rosemary Stallone, Sales Manager, Motorola, Inc.

"After reading *Are You For Real?!*, I understand that being me, just being me, honest and open-minded, gives me the much-needed tools for success."

— Gloria Bell, Author of
Healing Yourself Made Simple

"Procrastination is so me. So when I was asked, "Are you for real?" I guess the honest answer was 'No,' but reading David's book has made me want to change that."

— David Armstrong, Author of
Messages from the Spirit World

"Anytime in the past when I've discussed business and sales issues with David, he was able to cut through the noise and help me zero in. Now he will do the same for you in his new book *Are You For Real?!* His practical advice and introspective questions will make you rethink what you're doing, streamline your operations, and create winning strategies to keep you at the top of your game. I'm going to recommend this book to every salesperson I know."

— Mark Marmurstein,
President of Twin America

"It is about time we got this knowledge out of David's head and into print! If you work in sales, you need to read this book."

— Ken Barrows, Vice President,
Leisure Pass North America, LLC

"An authentic REAL life story of inspiration, persistence, and celebration of the freedom to succeed against all odds. Impressive, engaging, and highly recommended!"

— Rosemary McCormick, President,
Shop America Alliance

"After managing and leading top sales teams for over twenty years, I can honestly say *Are You For Real?!* is a must read for anyone in sales. I've had the honor and privilege of working with David in the past. He works with the utmost integrity, is beyond passionate about sales, and is one of the kindest and funniest people I know. Coach Stern is for real! He will help you get results."

— Diane Polnow, Former Director of
Business Development, American Express,
and President/Owner, DEP Consulting

"My income has been the same for the last seven years. After reading this book, I have hopes that working the ideas mentioned will help me increase my sales annually."

— Elisa Hawkinson, Author of *Calming Your Chaos*

"Between David Stern's heart-wrenching tale of how his father went from surviving the Holocaust to pursuing the American Dream and his own ingenious strategies for winning over customers, *Are You For Real?!* holds something for everyone who wants to succeed in sales and in life. Every page of this book is real, and you'll be turning to it again and again for advice and inspiration!"

— Tyler R. Tichelaar, Ph.D., and Award-Winning Author of *The Children of Arthur* series

"This powerful book is a "salesman's best friend." Chock-full of realistic and easy-to-implement concepts, practical hands-on tools, and street-smart wisdom, it offers everything you need to become a champion in selling."

— Susan Friedmann, CSP, International Best-Selling Author of *Riches in Niches: How to Make it BIG in a small Market*

"David Stern gets to the source of reality in his new book *Are You For Real?!*

David's insightful analogies and probing questions uncover the real authentic characteristics people need at their cores to achieve their lifelong goals. He digs to the root cause of people's actions and holds them accountable for what they say and do.

"As an owner of a ninety-four-year-old, three-generation-family flooring business, I found that David made me stop to think about how we interact with our clients every day, and he made me re-evaluate how we can adapt his incredible techniques and questions to our own business. His insight is truly valuable and creative in his approach to selling, and we will implement that approach right away in our sales staff and day-to-day business goals.

"*Are You For Real?!* is truly a must read for anyone who owns a business or is in any kind of sales profession."

— Dean Paulson, Vice President, Paulson Enterprises

ARE YOU FOR REAL?!

Going from Excuses to
Authentic Selling and
Living Your Dreams

DAVID STERN

AVIVA
PUBLISHING
New York

Are You For Real?!
Copyright © 2015 David Stern

Published by:

Aviva Publishing
Lake Placid, NY
518-523-1320
www.avivapubs.com

Address all inquiries to:

David Stern
1491 E 18th Street
Brooklyn, NY 11230
(917) 974-4547
david@coachstern.com
www.CoachStern.com

Printed in the United States of America.

978-1-943164-23-3 (softcover)
978-1-943164-24-0 (hardcover)
978-1-943164-25-7 (ebook)

Library of Congress Control Number: 2015909027

Jacket Design: www.AngelDogProductions.com
Interior Design: www.AngelDogProductions.com
Front Cover Design: Deer Design Brooklyn, NY
Editor: Tyler Tichelaar

First Edition

ACKNOWLEDGMENTS

Thank you to the following people for helping me in my personal and career paths:

Amy Begel, Chaim Beigel, Lorne Behrman, Edie Elias Boxstein, Tom Carroll, David Eastis, Kristen Esposito, Nicole Gabriel, Sam Goldstein, Vincent Guerra, Kent Gustavson, Towru Ikeda, Rabbi Naftali Horowitz, Hershel Jacobowitz, David Katz, Gisela Laufer, Bruce Lloyd, Terry Murphy, Yankel Posen, Belinda Plutz, Jennifer Powers, Herman Schreiber, Judith Stern, Patrick Snow, Rosemary Lockwood Stallone, Tyler Tichelaar, and Kevin Young

CONTENTS

PREFACE
LEARNING TO FISH EARLY

"Give a man a fish and you feed him for a day;
teach a man to fish and you feed him
for a lifetime."

— Maimonides

"When I was fifteen, I was the richest kid in Brooklyn."

— *David Stern*

I was incredibly bored growing up. In the area of Brooklyn where I lived, in the late '50s and early 1960s, our family didn't own a television, record player, videos, or any such form of entertainment. When the other kids and I came home from school, we didn't play punch ball (a game like baseball, but without the bats). We weren't involved in *any* sports or outside activities. Nothing.

What did that leave for us? Life for kids in my community was all about studying, studying, and more *studying*. I *hated* studying; it bored me. I would do anything to avoid doing my homework, which is when I started to watch my mother more closely. I quickly became inspired by her skills as a salesperson.

Before I was born, my father held down as many as three jobs at a time, doing anything he could to make a living. Then, after a few years, he and my mother started a rug import business, where my father was involved in managing operations, and my mother was the salesperson.

Growing up, I had no idea how hard my father had

worked to be successful. I had no idea of the obstacles he had overcome just to arrive as an immigrant on the shores of the United States. As a child, he would tell me about his parents and his sisters, but I never fully understood why I could never meet them. Not until I was an adult, as I'll relate later in this book, did I fully understand what it meant that he was a Jewish immigrant and a Holocaust survivor. As a child, I only knew that he was a hardworking man and content to let my mother have the limelight as the family business's salesperson.

The thing about my mother is, not only is she incredibly good with people, but she is lightning fast, and stealthy enough that, most of the time, we didn't even notice she had been gone on a sales trip! Between breakfast and dinner, she could be in Pittsburgh and Cleveland, and then back, all in the same day, without us kids knowing she had gone anywhere.

She always told us stories about visiting customers on the road. My favorite story is the one she told us about her most difficult prospect. This was a prospective client in Boston, and he always showed her the door. Year after year, each time she came to prospect this account, he got rid of her. Finally, one day he told her, "Mrs. Stern, if you weren't a woman, I would physically pick you up and *throw* you out!"

A few years later, after continued persistence, and her

amazing salesmanship and product demonstration, she landed him as a client, and netted a $25,000 or-der—which was a fortune in those days. She just didn't take "no" for an answer. In time, I would realize I had inherited her persistence.

The Richest Kid in Brooklyn

Like my fellow students back in the day, I always wanted some extra pocket money. I mean, what kid didn't want some money for *this* or *that*—whether it be penny candy or some kind of new toy. Eventually, it dawned on me—in order to get more money, I would have to earn it. With my mother's example in mind, I thought maybe the best way to earn the pocket change I wanted was to go into business.

Like I said earlier, homework bored me *stiff*. So each week, I would pick up the weekly local paper and read it from cover to cover, even the "want ads" in the back. Anything was better than homework.

In the want ads, I started to notice that people in the area were looking to buy or sell used refrigerators or other kitchen appliances. In the 1960s, people didn't buy appliances like they do today; they sold their old ones in order to fund the new ones. After a bit of inves-tigation, I decided I would become a "matchmaker," bringing together the sellers and buyers of appliances.

Thus began my first company. I saved some money and invested in a "record-a-call" machine (which was really high-tech back then, but it was basically an answering machine). I called NY Telephone and lied about my name, pretending I was my father, and I ordered a new phone line that I installed in my bedroom. I hid the phone really well, and I connected it up to the record-a-call. Then, I started placing ads in the local paper. The answering machine picked up the messages, and I brokered the deals. Within six months, I became the richest kid in Brooklyn.

I never could have pulled off my first business venture without one person: my mother. She found out pretty quickly what I was doing, but she didn't seem to mind too much. For a while, everything worked great.

When customers would call my new number, the phone never rang because it went right into the record-a-call, which was set to a low volume. I'd come home from school and my four brothers and my sister would be studying and doing their homework, oblivious to my bustling enterprise.

I would immediately go into my bedroom to listen to the messages and return calls. I would tally my new clients and figure out the scope of new deals. It was a blissful time.

Sales, wheeling and dealing, gave me freedom. It allowed me to earn at my own pace and save some money. Some months, I made more than a $150, which made me feel wealthy and successful. To put that into perspective, at the time, a generous (monthly/weekly) allowance of pocket change from my parents was between a nickel and a dime. If I had a quarter, chances are I stole it.

Things were going smoothly until one day I got busted. The deal was set: the seller would drop off the appliance in my parents' yard, and the buyer would come pick it up. But the buyer never showed up, leaving a monstrosity of a kitchen appliance inexplicably sitting in my parents' backyard.

When my father came home from work, he saw stuff in the yard he called "junk," and he asked my mother what was going on. After my mother told him what I was doing, he came upstairs and yanked the phone line out of the wall. My father believed that young kids should be studying rather than working in business. Just like that, I was out of business. But my excitement about sales—and wheeling and dealing—remained. *That* he couldn't yank out of me.

Forty Years in Business

As you can tell, my ambitions lay outside of the classroom. I barely managed to graduate high school and earn a diploma. Upon graduation, some of my fellow classmates chose to pursue a higher education, but at eighteen, I chose to join the workforce.

First, I decided to work in a local bank where I became the first Orthodox Jewish boy who had ever been a teller there. I worked every day from eight in the morning to four in the afternoon, and after six months, the bank decided to promote me and send me to school to learn more about the business. I was excited about the opportunity. I learned the basics of banking, but I found the parts about customer interaction especially fascinating. That aspect allowed me to focus on sales and helping others for the first time.

Three years later, a colleague and I wrote a manual to use when opening up a bank branch in a new community. I'm proud to say that manual is still in use in the Chicago library where the Federal Savings and Loan Insurance Corporation (FSLIC) is located. During this time, I was rising up the corporate ladder, moving swiftly from head teller, to platform assistant, to assistant branch manager, to, finally, holding an elected office as vice president of the branch.

My favorite aspect of the job was interacting with clients. Clients got to know me, I got to know them, and they started referring other customers to me. That was when I learned the importance of referrals in business. Taking good care of customers brings new customers. I became good at it, and I really took pride in my work. The feeling of helping others get what they want or need is worth more than just a paycheck.

Eventually, I got recruited to another bank that was planning to open a branch in Brighton Beach, Brooklyn. Within the first year, we earned $65 million in new CD deposits—breaking the bank's all-time record for deposits in a new branch. That was surely a milestone moment for me.

It's been forty joyous years since my clandestine backyard appliance operation and my fascination with my mother's superhero-like sales life. What a journey it has been! I have sold to individuals, mom and pop stores, department stores, chain stores, and corporate America. I have trained well over 14,000 salespeople in the business of selling and its benefits. I have represented and built an immigrant American, family-owned, successful business in over twelve countries—and I'm not done yet.

You're next...that's why you're reading this book—to learn about how to be the best salesperson and entrepreneur you can be, and I'm going to show you how.

David Stern

David Stern

INTRODUCTION
BEING AUTHENTIC

"The privilege of a lifetime is being who you are."

— Joseph Campbell

Are You For Real?!

It's both a question and an exclamation: "Are you for real?!" It has become a pet phrase of mine that I ask both the attendees of my sales seminars and my clients participating in my one-on-one coaching intensives. Sometimes, I'll ask the question with a wrinkled brow and an exasperated tone. Other times, I'll ask it while feeling inspired to get people into self-development, knowing that they will grow in their chosen careers. All the time, I'm seeking to help them realize their potentials.

These pages are filled with what I have learned from forty years of selling experience in the field, on the road, on the streets, at home, and at work. It's important to know about the business of selling, but it's just as important to get inside of what being a salesperson (and being a good and healthy person) is all about.

This book was written for you and for all who have chosen this path. This book is for those of you who are in sales and choose to knock on doors to earn a living. This book is for those of you who have made the decision not to work at a job from nine-to-five every day. If you are selling airplanes, automobiles, financial services, groceries, and if your income is based on a commission or salary plus commission, this book is for you. If you need to generate income for yourself or your family day after day, this book is for you.

Don't get me wrong; the stories and concepts throughout the book aren't just for salespeople. I have coaching clients who aren't in sales at all, and this book is for them, too. The universal idea is that change from within is worthwhile. So, if you are a corporate business executive, a truck driver, a secretary, or a farmer—this book is about living a better life by reaching toward and achieving your personal and career expectations. The two will go hand-in-hand when you are *for real*.

The Big Picture

Let's face it: most salespeople want to get rich. They want to earn the most money possible—and that makes sense. But what I have seen time and time again is that salespeople often jump the gun and want to earn a fortune before they get a view of the overall business of sales. Before you achieve the fortune, you need to have goals that are specific, measurable, achievable, realistic, and timed. I like to think of these goals as a puzzle. If you take the time to study and look at the big picture on the cover of the puzzle box, then study each piece carefully, you will effectively be able to sort it out. Only then can you properly put the pieces together.

Imagine a faraway picture of the professional life you desire to have. This book will help you look at the picture on that mental-image puzzle box, and then sort the disparate puzzle pieces into shapes, sizes, colors, and patterns. You will pick out the foundational pieces with four corners, start to put together the lines around the edges, and slowly, the image of the life you have always wanted will emerge.

If you have ever worked on a puzzle, you know that it takes quite a bit of time and effort to go through these steps. You have to put the work in. And it all begins when you ask yourself the question, *"Are you for real?!"*

For many years, I have traveled all across this great country and to many countries in Europe and South America, representing various products and services. I have had the opportunity to meet with thousands of salespeople. Whether they are selling products or services for a small company in South America, or a large company in New York, sales and marketing people inspire me, and I'm always curious to find out more about their jobs. In other words, meeting *you* out there on the same path as I am on has given me strength, despite the ups and downs of a life in sales.

Being in sales is not easy. It's challenging to make ends meet by wheeling and dealing. Sometimes, the challenges lie within the companies we work for. Maybe they don't give us proper training so we really don't know *how* to represent their products or services effectively.

But what's actually often lacking is *within* us. And it's about time to *get real*.

———

33

My Journey to Freedom

Seven years ago, I was in a dilemma that led to some profound life transformations. At the time, I represented a great company, traveled to many countries each year, was compensated well for my efforts, brought great results to the business, met the most fascinating and diverse people, built some great relationships worldwide, *but*—and here is the key—I was unhappy with the way upper management treated me and my colleagues.

In 2006, while on a business trip to Spain, I made the fateful decision to leave the company. But before I could leave, I needed to envision what was next, so I spent the next few years scouting and exploring new opportunities while continuing my work for this company. I didn't want to be impulsive and make a change without a solid plan. I needed to change the picture on the outside of the puzzle box: I chose new goals and painted the completed picture with the pieces in my mind's eye.

I thoroughly prepared for this radical shift in my life. I worked on my time management. In most of my spare time, I talked to people and researched different areas of opportunity. Finally, I landed on the path that would bring me into the future: sales and personal success coaching.

It was a satisfying path, both financially and in terms of helping others. I saw freedom and personal satisfaction on this path. Once I had that full picture on the puzzle box, all I had to do was piece together the life I envisioned. The thought of this new direction brought about a purposeful peace, and relief and excitement began to set in almost immediately. Now nothing could get in the way of my journey toward freedom, except my own self.

Next, it was just a waiting game. My annual consulting contract was about to expire and be renegotiated; decision time was on the horizon. After what would be my last business trip to San Francisco in that era of my life, instead of coming directly home to New York, I diverted my trip to Arizona to participate in what was, essentially, a conference on personal success.

The conference lodgings were stunning, the weather was balmy, and the few thousand participants from all over the world seemed blissful. But I was knotted up tightly with doubt, fear, worries, and anxiety. It had been three and a half years since that epiphanic moment of change, and now here I was about to put my dreams into action, but I was miserable and stressed.

I soaked up the many inspiring speaker sessions at the event. One speaker in particular, Mr. Terry Murphy, really impressed me. In his speech, he illuminated a connection between success in business and personal growth. His speech had a powerful impact on me, so I decided to reach out to him. While waiting to speak with him, I surveyed my life, reflecting back on my personal and professional journey and thinking about my current life changes. All of my emotions were in my eyes and on the tip of my tongue.

Our discussion exuded a mystical aura. I came in troubled and searching, but he was calm, wise, and asked me powerful questions. What we discussed and what I heard in that forty-five minute conversation was unbelievable.

He was a tall gentleman, and peering over me, he looked at the top of my head and saw my yarmulke. He told me that he understood everything I said, admired my courage and due diligence, and then explained that now it was a waiting game. Then he asked: "What does your *God* think? Why don't you tell Him your troubles and let Him resolve it? Pray for Him to make the decision and leave it to Him."

It was an exhilarating and intense meeting, and I left it feeling like a load had been lifted from my shoulders. I took his suggestion to heart, proceeded to play one of my best golf games ever, and ended up thoroughly enjoying the rest of the convention.

My mission had been cemented. I would help salespeople help themselves. *That* was my next career move.

This new era for me began quickly and vibrantly. Previously, I had studied and become a certified business coach, so it didn't take long to find a few clients and build a part-time practice. Soon, my income climbed to what I had been earning in my sales consulting position at the previous company. That was over five years ago. Since then, I've never looked back. Over the years, I have developed a rigorous training method that works, and I have the great joy of waking up each day to a thriving coaching career where I help better people's personal and professional lives.

The most glaring deficiency I see in my coaching clients is that they don't know the basics of a career in sales—they can't see the image on the cover of the puzzle box, and they can't identify the key corner puzzle pieces that will help them frame the whole picture. They have absolutely no training in self-development, database and time management, goal setting, etc.

Another hurdle my clients face is the obstacle they put in front of themselves every time they make an excuse. Everyone wants to make a lot of money, and every single one of my clients believes in the promise of sales. But the excuses I hear are so frustrating. If these are things that you say, listen to yourself, and listen to me asking you, "Are you for real?!" What is your excuse? "I would sell more, but…." "I could make a million dollars next year, but…." "If I could only do _____, I would be a big success." Think about the things you say to yourself, and the things you tell your family and friends.

Now, instead of letting those excuses be your escape, come back to the puzzle metaphor and think about the big picture on the front of the puzzle box. When I stand in front of an audience, I ask those in attendance, "What does your puzzle look like? Is it the country house with a pool? Is it a new home with a two car garage? Sending your kids to an Ivy League college?"

Right now, your business is cluttered with a mess of pieces, but the big picture of what your life could be is there, and you can envision it. Once you have that big picture on the puzzle box, all that is left is fitting all the pieces together. In sales, there are many elements that help us do this, including building relationships, time and database management, prospecting, properly timed follow-ups, product knowledge, and developing the right skill set to treat a career in sales as it should be: *a business.*

In this book, I will teach you these sales career essentials and share enlightening life and work lessons from my four decades in sales. It's my hope that I can bring you the calm focus that Mr. Terry Murphy brought me years ago, when I was at my life journey crossroads.

AUTHENTIC SELLING TIPS

1. Envision what is next for your career. You can't get anywhere if you don't know where you're going.
2. Stop making excuses for why you can't succeed and address your fears. Work on your personal transformation and you will see it translate into your career transformation.

FREEDOM QUESTIONS

1. Too often we allow our minds to become our prisons. Instead, we want to move from fear to freedom. If nothing stood in your way, what would be the big picture you would want for your life?

_____

_____

_____

_____

_____

2. What are some goals you can set today that will serve as puzzle pieces so you can begin to put that big picture together?

_____

_____

_____

_____

_____

3. What are your excuses that always seem to keep you from achieving those goals? Be honest with yourself.

_____

_____

_____

_____

_____

_____

4. Are you willing to quit making excuses? What is the one thing you will commit to doing today to overcome your excuses and move toward your goals?

_____

_____

_____

_____

_____

_____

CHAPTER ONE

ESCAPING THE 9 TO 5 GRIND

"The difficulty lies not so much in developing
new ideas as in escaping from old ones."

— John Maynard Keynes

"I was in an $86 a week prison—I did my time from 8:30 in the morning 'til 4:30 in the evening."

— *David Stern*

W hen I was a bank teller, I was part of the nine-to-five grind. My workday started at 8:30 a.m. and ended at 4:30 p.m. Many times throughout each day, I stared out the window, longing to be part of the hustle and bustle of the street. Being confined to an office setting felt stifling in so many ways.

I wasn't earning much at this bank job. My paycheck was about $86 a week, before taxes. After taxes, I could perhaps buy a couple of hot dogs, a soda, and, if I were lucky, a potato knish.

I liked the interaction with customers, though. I loved people coming and going. Every few minutes there was another customer. They all wanted the same basic things—to cash checks and make deposits. I liked giving them good service, but the whole thing was so routine. I felt stagnant doing the same thing day in and day out. I felt like a prisoner of the nine-to-five system.

Is It Worth It?

Working environment aside, I remained steadfast in my ambitions to excel in the business world. I graduated from the world of being a teller and went on to become assistant branch manager. To further my reach, I went back to school, somehow fitting in three hours of class three times a week between fulltime work and domestic life.

It all paid off. Soon I became a vice president at the bank, but I quickly realized that the money wasn't that much greater than my earnings as an assistant branch manager. I was told that in three to five years, I could max out at $500 a week, which would be roughly $25,000 a year— not too bad for a young man in the early '70s on a job.

But being confined to a set salary, even a higher paying one, made me feel trapped. No matter how hard I worked, it was somebody else setting the limits on how much I could earn.

When the particular bank I was working for opened a new branch in another area in Brooklyn, I was relocated as branch manager. I made it my mission for my new branch to be a huge success. But no matter how hard I worked, my income flat-lined at $25,000. There was no commission or reward for promoting and encouraging hard work. Looking back, there should have been an incentive to bring in more business while growing the bank's clientele and financial profile.

The lack of opportunity to better my financial life kept me thinking, "Is it worth it?" The days were a grind: getting up at six o'clock in the morning, preparing myself for the day, having breakfast, and braving the morning rush hour commute. At 8:30 a.m., I clocked in, at 12:00 p.m. or so, I got my hour lunch break, and then I was released around 4:30 or 5:00 p.m. Most of the time throughout the day, I always had a boss breathing down my neck. No matter how high up in the ranks you climb, everyone has to answer to someone in the nine-to-five world. The "This is all there will ever be" feeling started depressing me. Every day, I kept looking longingly outside, feeling that somehow there was freedom in those streets.

I don't want to belittle a life in retail, banking, or really any nine-to-five career. It's an admirable route for most people because it offers stability, especially if you have a family to provide for. In my position, there were some great perks, and those helped me figure out where my heart was and how I wanted to pivot my career in order to grow as a professional and as a person.

What I liked about my retail banking position as assistant branch manager was that, on occasion, it allowed me to go out to community events and senior citizen centers when the bank hosted breakfasts, lunches, and dinners. I enjoyed this community outreach. I would attend these gatherings to discuss the banking opportunities available to the senior demographic. The idea was that the personal touch would help bring people into the bank to open up accounts. For me, the merit of the work was seeing the smiles on the potential customers' faces. There's no greater satisfaction than that.

The time I spent out in the field, doing meaningful work and bringing in business, felt great. I liked being out on the streets instead of daydreaming from an office window. I felt free. More and more, I dreaded sitting behind a desk in an office all day long.

My banking career ended in a non-dramatic way. I relocated to California to explore another, potentially more lucrative, banking opportunity. However, I am of the Jewish faith and, up until the point of my move, I would make myself available to work Sundays instead of Saturdays if needed, so I could observe Sabbath. The banks I worked at also kept this schedule, so it never was an issue. In 1978, the banking regulators changed laws and allowed banks to be open on Saturdays. In California, my new position required that I work Saturdays, or be available in case of emergency, but I couldn't do that.

That was the end of my banking career. It was also my release from the daily nine-to-five grind. It was my chance to seize the opportunity to go out and find something else more satisfying. It's been forty years since that pivotal moment.

The J-O-B

You may have noticed that this chapter is about freedom and autonomy. It answers the question: Why Sales? In short, there are many answers. People in sales get to experience the seasons, breathe fresh air, and exist without the boss-to-employee—and sometimes dictator-to-employee—relationship. Additionally, there are incentives to working hard and bringing in business. You can make your own hours so you're released from the rush-hour scramble. At its most fundamental level, leaving the nine-to-five grind behind is about taking control of your destiny.

Selling is a business, not a job, and it offers accomplishments and success beyond a job's parameters. Continue reading this book and I will enlighten you about the possibilities of sales and ground you with the realities of the path.

My old friend, Mr. Kevin Young, used to say the word "JOB" stands for Just-Over-Broke. At a job, you are paid just enough so you don't quit, and you work just hard enough so you don't get fired. Within this "boxed in" paradigm, it's hard to get ahead and have goals. What if you want to buy a home? What if you want to send your kids to a better school? How about that dream vacation? What if, heaven forbid, someone has a medical emergency and you need to cover extra out-of-pocket expenses?

You have dreams and you want to grow, but you're contained by the four prison walls of the given salary and the demands of the job. You're "just over broke," and you may be wasting your time in a career prison. When you're working a job, or you're working for someone, generally speaking, there's a ceiling of how much you can earn. Whatever it is, whether its $25,000, $50,000, or $500,000, that's it. Maybe the company will give you a few percent extra as a raise, and every once in a blue moon, you might get a little bonus, but you can't make more than what the given parameters are. The cost of living expenses always rises, which is, frustratingly, out of sync with the salary ceiling of working for someone and waiting for a raise.

Freedom Has a Price

My father had three jobs because one job didn't cut it. He worked all three on a daily basis in order to put food on the table. It was no way to live. So my parents ended up starting a business selling machine-made oriental rugs. By starting their own business, they broke out of their nine-to-five prison and freed themselves from the drudgery of three jobs.

In sales, you can earn a lot of money, but you really have to understand how to be your own boss because you still have the responsibilities to pay bills and take care of your family.

Freedom has a price. And as I write this, I think about how many years I've been on the road; every once in awhile, I slept in the car in a parking lot to be up early for an appointment. It wasn't easy. But you know what? It felt good to be autonomous; it felt good to enjoy the changes in the weather; and it still feels good to know that when you run a sales business, you'll never experience a heart-wrenching layoff—there is a unique angle of job security in sales.

When you're an employee working for someone else, sometimes you live in fear of layoffs. Especially today, job security while working in an office doesn't exist. Corporate culture has changed. It used to be that you worked for a company for many years, and at retirement, the company threw you a party and gave you a gold watch. Throughout your tenure at the company, benefits were the added bonus, and maybe you got your family a good health plan and a robust 401K package. But this model hardly exists anymore.

We live in a new era. It is an era of downsizing, reduced benefits, layoffs, venture capitalism, overseas relocation, and financially lean startup companies. It's scary out there. I am not saying that there aren't great companies you can work for where you can earn good money. There are, BUT how much can you earn there? Here is a better question: Could you earn more than the managers?

In sales, you are the boss; you're working for yourself—so you'll never get laid off. But you have to be properly trained in personal development and understand sales from a gut level. If you don't learn about yourself and try to get better, what are the long-term chances that you will succeed?

Success in sales comes down to some fundamentals that include having a good attitude, building relationships, believing in the products or services you sell, and investing in yourself to be the best you can be. Embracing these fundamentals makes you an asset to your business (and your family), and the only person who can fire you is *you*.

Sure, you live on a roller coaster of financial ups and downs, but you can have some fun riding it. If you pay attention to the daily requirements of working in the selling business, you can be in control of your financial destiny. Sounds scary, right? It could be if you don't know what you are doing.

The Sky's the Limit

One of the biggest problems I had adjusting to my new life in sales was understanding that I didn't have the cushion of a salary. When you have a punch-clock job, you can always rely on that weekly chunk of change. You have a great week, you get amount "X." You have a horrible week, you get amount "X." So no matter what, you can support your bottom line. Now, all of a sudden, you are walking out of the nine-to-five grind, you are free, but you have to start at sum zero and create sales to fund a minimum bottom line. You could earn $200, $2,000, or even more per week.

It took a little acclimatization, but as I made my way out there in sales, I started to feel this confidence, this feeling of "I can do this." Of course, part of me still craved the comfort of the nine-to-five life—the safety net of the salary and the familiarity of the firm schedule. It's easy to live this life. However, the further you get from that stifling career path, the freer you get, and the more opportunities you have. And that's what I live for. I live for the opportunity to earn what I want to earn—to be able to work hard, build my business, work for myself, and feel good inside because I have accomplished something.

When I started in sales, I was told: "David, the sky's the limit for how much you can earn." I asked myself: "How do I reach the sky?" Well, I learned you build a ladder, you get a solid foundation in the business of selling, and from there, it's all up to you. Selling is freedom. You can earn as much as you want, as long as you do the right thing. In my move from office work to sales, I immediately doubled my income—I busted through the ceiling of how much money I could earn.

Learning Fast

I started my sales career in the gold jewelry industry. I got involved with a company based in New York. The manager, Mr. Yankel Posen, offered me a fifteen-year-old established territory in California and other Western states. He explained that if I learned the ropes from the previous salesperson, I could really do well. I saw the green light, but I didn't know how to drive through it.

I needed to know the basics. Besides the products, and the built-in customer base, I needed to understand the time management that mapped out this territory since what I inherited was big. I also had to work on database management to capitalize on leads and avoid dead-ends.

Every trade has its tools—if you're a carpenter, you need to know about hammers, screwdrivers, drills, and how to use them. I needed to learn the tools of the trade of selling, and I didn't have a teacher or a coach. I had Lou Hirsch, the gentlemen who had the territory before me, and since he was ill in Las Vegas, I had to spend time there for him to show me the ropes. He managed to teach me a little about how to work a territory in an effective and efficient way. He taught me that the number one thing in sales is you build relationships. The better you get at it, the more people will respect you, which will put them in a better position to buy from you. Besides his guidance, I had to go out there to practice on my own and learn. To stay free and take advantage of this opportunity, I needed to learn fast.

Getting Out There

The most important thing I learned early on was that if I didn't go out to work, I wasn't going to be earning any money. If I didn't go visit any clients or prospects and present them with my wares, I wasn't going to earn any money. There were no paid sick days or mental health days. I always needed to be in front of clients or prospects. For me, it was great because I love people. I love talking to people. I love working with people. I love showing people products and services that will improve their lives or income.

I learned that you have to care about the people you are selling to. Remember, it's not just about you; it's about them—they give you the time of day. If you are compassionate, you should be asking: "What can I do for your business, for your family? How can I help you with your needs?" You have to listen deeply to your prospective customers; you have to care because otherwise you're selfish, and nobody wants to work with a selfish business person.

There is nobility in a life in sales. Despite some of the

stereotypes, successful salespeople are sincere and heartfelt. When it comes down to it, a sales business is based on relationships and honesty. You have to build relationships with people so they feel good about purchasing from you. And the core of any solid and healthy relationship is trust. You can be trustworthy only when you believe and understand the product or service you are offering. You have to believe in your soul that there is a need for the product, and if you know it inside and out, you can show people how it will improve their lives.

"No" Means "Yes" (Eventually)

It's unrealistic to create an image of the business of sales without explaining the complexity of hearing the word "No" a million times. Who feels good about hearing "No"? Don't take it personally. I've learned to look at it this way: "No" means "Not now, maybe later." With a smile on your face, good database management and follow-up, you can come back three or more months later to get a possible "Yes."

When someone gives you a "Yes," he's saying yes to you because he likes you and the way you are looking to help him. People don't really care too much about the company you represent, although it could also be important. You have established trust, and you have shown them how the product or service will satisfy a need. You exude confidence. Your business depends on possessing unwavering confidence. You can't be afraid or tentative because you're reeling from setbacks. You need to project confidence and self-assurance at all times.

The Roller Coaster Effect

One of the most common erosions of confidence is what I alluded to before: "the roller coaster" effect. A life in sales is just like being on a roller coaster because we go up and down, but no matter what, we have to hang on. Don't lose your confidence if things don't go your way for a few days or weeks. Remember, when the train that takes you to the top suddenly drops, it comes down with such speed that it goes right back up again, and that's what you're hanging on for. You have to accept that you're going to go up and down. It's a way of life, and you just have to hang on and remember when you're going down that you'll go back up again.

If the trend continues down, however, you have to be honest with yourself. Maybe it's time to rethink your strategy, your general approach, or reevaluate your goals. Change is extremely difficult, but we have to allow ourselves the opportunity to change. Look deep within yourself, be honest, and decide which habits contribute to your accomplishments and which ones hold you back from success.

I clearly remember when I went to a class on self-development that the instructor handed out little mirrors on a handle.

I asked, "What's this? Why are you giving us this mirror?"

His response to the group was, "Look at *yourselves*."

I said, "Okay, I'll look at myself; so now what?"

He asked, "What do you see?"

I said, "Well, I've got two eyes and a nose."

"No, no, no. How about looking deeper? What are your desires, your goals? What is it that's going on with you? How are you living? How are you communicating? What is it about you that you might change so you can live a better life? What sort of changes might you need to make in order to achieve the goals and dreams you want to happen?"

This introspection is powerful stuff, but here is something I want to add right now: You don't have to be that intense all the time. Sometimes, I like to play a game of golf midday; I just make sure I account for this in my time management. It is crucial to relax and recharge in order to maintain the hectic and exciting pace of this lifestyle.

A Passion for Sales

When I reflect back to the nine-to-five life I had years and years ago, I know I needed that experience. I learned some important interpersonal skills. Most importantly, I learned what I didn't want from life, and I have never regretted leaving that world behind. The air I breathe outside is much better, the autonomy emboldens my spirit, and the financial potential keeps me inspired and excited.

My dear friends, if you choose to live this lifestyle, go out and have a tremendous amount of fun doing it. There's work to do and there's a lot to learn, but there's also fun and reward. There's nothing like it. Forty years later, there's still nothing nicer and sweeter than meeting another person, getting to know him, finding out his goals or needs, or just making new friends. I never get tired of putting a smile on another's person's face.

Sales is my passion, and it's my life. Sales has taken me from selling jewelry to retailers to representing a giant in corporate America. Sales has taken me to different parts of the world, many times. I've been to many countries I never thought I would visit—dazzling places like Cannes, Monte Carlo, Amsterdam, Berlin, Brussels, Budapest, Acapulco, Rome, Rio, Buenos Aires, London, and many, many more. I've met so many wonderful people at business meetings, conventions, and social gatherings. For me, nothing is more exhil-

arating than spending time with other sales professionals, listening to them and sharing ideas and ways
of selling. I've also had the opportunity to experience
exotic cultures, eat great food, and bring my wife, who
is my best friend, along for the ride sometimes. This
is what I call living. There is nothing like the freedom
afforded by a life in sales.

AUTHENTIC SELLING TIPS

1. A life in sales is about autonomy. It's freedom from stuffy and stagnant offices. It's a chance to breathe fresh air, experience the seasons, and meet new and exciting people daily.

2. There is no financial ceiling in sales—it's all up to you what you earn.

3. Working for yourself offers job security that corporations cannot offer in this era of layoffs, company relocations, downsizing, and startups.

FREEDOM QUESTIONS

1. What has your JOB taught you about what you don't want in life?

_____

_____

_____

_____

_____

_____

2. What habits do you have that have helped you to be successful?

_____

_____

_____

_____

_____

_____

_____

3. How can you use those habits to your greater advantage?

_____

_____

_____

_____

_____

_____

4. What habits do you have that are holding you back from success?

_____

_____

_____

_____

_____

5. Below write down the worst bad habit you have and then write what you will commit to doing to change it into a habit to aid you in your success.

_____

_____

_____

_____

_____

CHAPTER TWO
GETTING DISTRACTED

"It's amazing how confused and distracted
and misdirected so many people are."
— Stephen Covey

"I was living the dream,
but soon it began to catch up to me."

— *David Stern*

In 1983, I was living in California, representing a New York based jewelry manufacturer in the Golden State and in the surrounding five Western states. It was a prosperous time financially—the bills were paid; more than that, I was accumulating a little nest egg of savings. I was living the dream, but soon it began to catch up to me.

On the surface, it felt like a blissful time. I had a thriving social life, I was making a lot of new friends, and I was traveling to wonderful places. It was a new life for me, something I could hardly imagine with my Brooklyn frame of reference. But the good times began to overtake my life because they felt better than the actual work.

When I look back at myself circa 1983, I can see I was lacking some personal development fundamentals. I was enraptured with the lifestyle of the hustle, and not focused on the big picture of my journey as a person and as an ambitious professional. I could have maximized my relationships and my career by reaching out to bigger clients and taking on more challenging opportunities. I could have progressed to high-end products and engaged with powerhouse companies. But I became imprisoned by my lifestyle; I was scared to break out of the cushy life I was leading. I wasn't for real.

Looking back, I realize I didn't have anyone who could have helped me. I wasn't exposed to personal-development, life coaches, or sales coaches. Truthfully, even if I had been, I am not sure I would have been receptive to that change or growth. I didn't have a vision for it.

Halcyon Years

The 1980s were a halcyon time for the jewelry business—at one point, gold reached $800 an ounce. The prices of gold fluctuated daily, with wild swings up and down; eventually, jewelry companies began to flounder and go belly up from this economic fluctuation. To stabilize, the convention of selling changed to value by weight. Because the company model I worked for stuck to a piece-based selling convention, it couldn't keep up. In time, it lost the market share, and instead of altering its business practice, the company also closed shop and I was out of a job. My world came crashing down.

It was a difficult pill to swallow. Yes, I had some money saved up to keep me going for a little while, but to change my environment and move back to New York City was humbling. I had this pride over leaving home, that classic "going West, gold rush" type of thinking. I felt like I had transcended so much with the move, and I felt like I was self-made.

Fears started creeping in as reality hit. I became consumed with fears and doubts—of losing my lifestyle and having to go back to New York with my tail between my legs. It seemed as if it were a defeat for me. I didn't think about my accomplishments or the opportunities I could leverage given my contacts and successes.

Back to the Grind

Returning to New York, I found myself listless, drifting through the days. I spent many a day looking for a sales job or opportunity, once again. I was offered a behind-the-counter sales job at a retail company. Since I wasn't in a very good space then and I don't like spending time doing nothing, I took the job, knowing full well that it meant going back to that nine-to-five grind I disliked so much. So instead of living off my savings, I preferred a paycheck and structure to my life until I could get back on my feet.

With this sales job, I found myself behind a counter, selling retail, to customers who came through the door. It was exactly what I didn't want to do—it was the life I had left behind years ago. Not very long after, I would say to myself, "I'm back in a rut again." Back to the routine: having breakfast at 7:30 in the morning, taking the jam-packed subway train into Manhattan, working from nine to six, and withering away in a dead-end retail sales job.

I dreaded going to work most of the time. I enjoyed the interaction with people while I was there, but I didn't enjoy much else about the position. After some time on the J-O-B, I started to act out my frustrations through slacking off. I stopped coming in at 9:00 sharp; soon it was 9:30, and then 10:00 and 10:30, and then I would always find an excuse to leave early.

One day, after a networking meeting with other salespeople, I had an epiphany: In order for me to break free of this shackling lifestyle, I needed to develop myself personally. I also needed to cultivate other strengths in the sales world. I had personal work to do in order to get back to doing business the way I was doing it in California, or even better. That meant knocking on doors and visiting people outside the four walls of an office or a store. I wanted to transcend the J-O-B path.

The Path to Personal Development

I soon found out, through a mentorship program, that personal development is the key. If you want to move into that higher end of selling, the Park Avenue of sales, so to speak, you have to do some serious introspection and make some changes. At that point, I realized that my California lifestyle—working through the day and going to nightclubs at night—was no longer good enough and wasn't going to work in this new era.

Knowing there was a way out—no matter how far off it seemed in terms of the personal work I had to do—gave me this glimmer of hope. It felt like waking up from a coma. Everything came into focus and felt new. Life was full of possibilities; freedom existed!

I kept the retail job because I needed the paycheck, but everything now felt different because I had a purpose. The mornings didn't seem that agonizing anymore. I knew my current situation was temporary, and I was on my way to a more fulfilling, and also more lucrative, life.

The mentorship program I decided to enroll in was exclusive and its platform was rigorous. My first interaction with a company rep was profound. It went something like: "Show up on time here, show me that you're for real and that you really, really want to get better, and make some changes. If you show me that, I will be here for you."

It was a life-changing time, and it re-scripted my foundational core as a person and a professional. It helped me get into that Park Avenue level of business I mentioned earlier. It ushered in a new time in my life as exciting as my California existence, but it was infinitely more fulfilling because I was living authentically. After one year of my hard personal work, I finally landed a sales job that changed my life and future career in sales.

Asking the Right Questions

I am going to be a little vulnerable here: Much of the turmoil of my story is derived from some lack of personal confidence. Lack of progress in life is often due to a lack of confidence that courses through your body, mind, and heart. It overtakes you. Many people go through life blind to this, but you picked up this book; therefore, I suspect that deep down you may be struggling with some of the same issues I grappled with.

I realized I had to rebuild myself from within. I am no different from you or anyone else. After experiencing and going through the personal success process I went through, and having the honor of meeting so many wonderful people and seeing so many beautiful places, I've realized how blessed I am, and now is the time to give back. I want to help other people achieve the same dreams and goals and obtain the same freedom I've received. Being a coach has become my life's work because it is the best way for me to relate to others and help other people achieve freedom. And I ask every new client what was previously asked of me: *Are you for real?!*

As a coach, I work with individuals and do intensive sessions with companies. The best way to help people is to understand them, so I ask a lot of questions. I ask about dreams, goals, and the nature of their work. I inquire about the products my clients are selling, how they attract customers, how long they've worked with the given product, how well they understand the benefits of their product, and how they structure their days. When companies work with me, it's because they want to increase productivity and performance, and the process begins the same way, with me asking a lot of questions.

Here is an example of a typical case. A salesperson comes in the door and says, "David, I'm earning $125,000 a year. I'm content with $125,000 a year, but I want to earn more. How do I do it?" What I do next is investigate the person's reasons for wanting to earn more: what are his or her possible new goals? I get to learn about the person's professional habits. I get a sense of his or her time management and database management, among other sales basics. I get to look at possible time wasters. Is my client taking long lunches? Is he regularly keeping in touch with his customers and leads in his database? Then, I have him describe some of his real-life prospecting scenarios.

Another client example is the person who is excellent at prospecting, but who lacks the confidence to schedule appointments with prospects. This person is crippled by internal fears—like the fear of rejection—or the nagging fear that he doesn't have solid product knowledge.

One of my clients told me that for three years she had been diligently pursuing the same leads, but the prospects consistently said no. My advice to her was to stay consistent. Many years ago, I was in the same situation, but I stayed the course and finally ended up selling to the company.

Recently, I worked with some sales partners, and we were role-playing their sales strategies. During our session, I realized they weren't asking the right questions and they didn't have strong listening skills. These two talents are complimentary; if you have both of these qualities, you can easily get to first base. The key is to listen to what the person is saying, and to be able to offer a solution.

Changing Little Habits

Sometimes, small changes have powerful repercussions. Maybe a person is overly aggressive or perpetually late. Changing little habits can drastically alter sales performance. All of these are linked—the personal and the professional—and the more we are open to change, the more we make ourselves open to success. It's really that simple.

The work and home connection can also be problematic in the opposite direction—poor performance on the job can really hurt family life. In this case, I will tell my clients that you could be chipping away at your relationship at home because you're not being the provider you're supposed to be: *Are you for real?!*

Let's address these fundamental issues outside of these examples in a blunt manner by asking you four questions:

1. **What is your confidence level in the morning?** You wake up, you have your breakfast, you brush your teeth, and you prepare for your day. Now, how much confidence do you have in the morning that you're going to achieve the goals that you set out for the day? In other words, how excited are you about getting going and having a great day?

2. **What about communication skills?** How well do you communicate? Are you always on top of your game with your interpersonal skills?

3. **If you're not moving forward, is it because of fear?** What's the fear? I find a lot of people fear change. If you're afraid to change, the only

thing that's going to happen is you're going to stay where you are, or even get worse.

4. **How well do you know your business?** Do you know how to set reasonable and achievable goals? How is your product knowledge? Do you ask for referrals? Do you understand how to build trust and present yourself authentically to your customers?

No one is perfect. I believe the only time I'm going to be perfect is when I'm six feet under. In life, we all make mistakes. So what? The important thing is to come to the table to learn and to be willing to make yourself better. Be more confident. Improve your communication skills. Be more excited about what you're doing. Be more present in plotting out ways to achieve your goals.

To withstand the sales roller coaster's ups and downs—times of making money and times of pinching pennies—you constantly have to be looking in the mirror and asking yourself: *Are you for real?!* Keep working on your self-development, your communication skills, your confidence, and your product knowledge. Do this and you will get through the roller coaster effect and be better equipped to go the distance with a life in sales.

I always want to get better, and I always have room to improve. I am resolved to do so because I'm not going back to a J-O-B situation. That's where I don't want to be. What about you?

Skyward View

In my life, I am reminded constantly of my path. Working with my clients always helps me reflect. The great city of New York puts my life into profound perspective. While walking the big streets of Manhattan with those tall buildings, I am reminded of how I used to look down. I was slumped over, sinking into the concrete, weighed down by my lack of accomplishments, by my negativity. Now when I walk those same streets, I look at the big buildings and am inspired by their skyward thrust. I'm not looking at my toes.

So when Barry or Suzie comes into my office and he or she says, "David, this is where I am," I can identify with where they are. I know they have families to support, they have dreams, and they want to feel accomplished as business people and as decent human beings. If they're bold enough to face their fears and become real, all that could happen for them. And if *you're* willing to become the real you, if you're willing to accept who you are and grow, then you are going to be able to make the next move.

As a coach, as a mentor, as an acting sales manager, or a consultant—all four different hats that I wear—

the most frustrating aspect of my role is when I feel or see how stubborn people are and how they're afraid to make the necessary changes.

Right now, I would like to circle back to the issues I presented earlier—the ones that imprison us and keep us from reaching our goals—and give you a comprehensive list of the most common ones. From my years as a coach, these are the biggies, the Top 10. I will explain each one below.

TOP 10 BAD HABITS THAT KEEP

PEOPLE FROM REACHING THEIR GOALS

1. Messiness and Disorganization

2. Poor Time-Management Skills

3. La-La Land vs. Focused Thinking

4. Poor Communication Skills vs. Focused Listening

5. Underestimating Personal Presence

6. Lack of Confidence

7. Poor Impulse Control

8. Not Setting Viable Goals

9. Not Being a Go-Getter

10. Unwillingness to Change

When you read these, keep in mind that understanding them doesn't have to be a negative experience. It's a positive thing to be aware of them. There is hope in change. If you know your issues, and work on them, it only benefits you, and you can only grow both in the business of selling and in your personal development. Think of this as the first step toward becoming the real you.

I firmly believe that many people don't understand the business of selling. Selling is not a job; it's a business. I want to give you insights to achieve. Let's now go through this Top 10 list and see what it has to do with the business of selling.

1. Messiness and Disorganization

A cluttered desk tells me that a person's very busy, which, in some instances, is excellent. She has a lot of incoming work, which has basically exploded on her desk. However, it also indicates that she could potentially be late to appointments or sound confused or rushed with her clients.

It's a wonderful thing to have so much work that it's hard to find time to keep things tidy. But a cluttered desk is not only an unnecessary inconvenience; it also represents a cluttered mind. In other words, you have so much going on that you begin to get sloppy in your professional life. You forget appointments, you show up late, or you get there on time out of breath from rushing, and then you make a chaotic first impression. Also, if you have a cluttered desk, it means crucial information is not readily accessible, so you're often going into transactions unprepared because you can't locate essential background information. All of this is important because it chips away at your credibility in your customers' eyes. Remember, your customers are your livelihood. You always want to appear composed and well informed.

If you're organized and you prioritize, you will also prevent emergency situations. By doing things when they need to be done, without allowing other things to disturb you, most of the time, you won't have an emergency. Instead, you will be relaxed, prepared, and you will never get yourself into situations that you cannot easily handle.

Put all the ducks in a row. Pace yourself in a systematic way and time yourself. Without disturbances, you're going to have better results, and feel better about what you're doing.

Having a cluttered desk, not having your database management properly organized, and having flawed priorities keeps you in that personal prison you have created; that's how you get stuck. By getting organized, having a clear vision, and knowing where things are at any given time, you will function in a more productive way, without frustration.

2. Poor Time-Management Skills

It's subtle how poor time-management skills can rear their ugly heads in our daily, professional lives, so I want to reveal these instances in a clear and candid fashion.

The first instance I would like to examine is being too available to others when you should be working. Now, there's nothing better and more wonderful than being the type of person who is willing to help your coworkers or colleagues. But, on the flipside, being available to others at inappropriate times takes you away from more important tasks. You need to set boundaries and be disciplined with time. Instead of dropping everything to help people every time, simply ask them to come back later. This practice still allows you to help others while putting your own priorities first.

Taking long lunches is another bad habit that hinders productivity. Sometimes salespeople go out with their coworkers or colleagues for lunch and they have discussions, which is a healthy activity. It's beautiful to discuss life and business and to collaborate with others in the same world—the insights are invaluable, and you get to have a meaningful connection with people who truly "get it." But "watch your calories" because sometimes we overextend the time allocated for lunch, and instead of forty-five minutes or an hour, we wind up with an hour and a half lunch. How many more calories are you taking in while you're doing all this? And how much time and money are you losing because you're not out there selling?

3. La-La Land vs. Focused Thinking

On a related topic, being present is vital to productivity and using your time wisely. Sometimes, I see people walking down the street who are clearly day-dreaming. They're in la-la land. Their heads are in a different state, in a different country. Be aware. Be awake. Smell the air. Smell the coffee. There's a saying: It's okay to build castles in the sky as long as you don't move in. Be careful when you're daydreaming. You can get lost there if you stay too long. Focused thinking is about paying attention to what's going on in the here and now. Don't think about what's going to happen next week, next month, next year, and miss what's happening in the moment. Be fully present in the here and now. Otherwise, time will run right by you, and you will miss the opportunities in front of you.

4. Poor Communication Skills vs. Focused Listening

Miscommunication, in its most basic form, stems

from a lack of clarity. Either you're not really listening to people, you're not clear about what you want to say, or some combination of the two. Listening is one life skill that can improve the quality of your business and your personal life.

Seventy percent of the time, success in sales comes down to listening. With customers, it is essential to understand their needs, wants, and desires, and also to be able to deliver a solution-based message they can understand if you want to make a sale.

Developing strong and clear communication skills will also deeply benefit many aspects of your life. Remember, it comes down to understanding people and being understood. Whether it's with your parents, your kids, your spouse, your business associate, or your friends, the ability to communicate effectively will help you no matter where you go, and no matter what you do.

Communication doesn't just mean talking. Some people seem to have good communication skills, but they exhaust you with nonstop talking. Being a good communicator means being able to listen and understand what the other person is saying—or not saying. Good communication is about the authentic connection we make, and that connection needs to extend to our personal and professional lives. If you're going to be in a good relationship with another person, you need to respect that person. You need to pay attention to him/her, listen to him/her, and understand what he/she feels, hears, and sees. Empathize with other people and you will become a great communicator because, at the most foundational level, people just want to be heard.

Building communication skills helps you expand your business network. You will grow socially and financially in business—life becomes richer in all aspects if you establish authenticity and realness in your interactions.

5. Underestimating Personal Presence

Your sheer physical presence sends a message to the public. Body language and appearance are communication skills in themselves. Consider, for example, something that salespeople do to cope with stress, like smoking. It's not only bad for your health, but when people meet you, you stink of smoke, which could put people off.

I quit smoking on September 25th, 1990, because the week before, when I arrived at a client's office, I overheard her say to her assistant, "Oh, Mr. Stern must be here because I smell the smoke. He always reeks of smoke." She didn't even need to see me to know I was there.

At the time, I smoked two to three packs a day. I gave

the same excuse every other smoker has given—smoking seemed to calm my nerves. But I began to realize that I was putting people off by smelling of cigarettes—people didn't want to be near me. Being clean and well-groomed attracts people.

6. Lack of Confidence

We all struggle with confidence—that's a constant. The variable is how we deal with it. There have been entire years when I have struggled with confidence.

Sometimes, a lack of confidence stems from not fully understanding a product or service you are working with. You build your confidence in this instance through immersing yourself in your work and really knowing the ins and outs of the product and service you are providing.

It may seem strange, but failures also build confidence because they implore you to figure out what you were doing wrong. The big message here is that essential customer-to-salesperson confidence begins with your own self-confidence.

7. Poor Impulse Control

In sales, the ability to control your impulses is paramount; otherwise, impulses too often manifest themselves in rash decisions. One example is agreeing to give a customer a price without first checking with management and the boss, or shortchanging yourself by settling too early on a lower price.

There's something between yes and no—it's that gray area that says, "Let me think about it." I learned about it thirty years ago when a mentor of mine approached me and said, "David, why does everything have to be a yes or a no, and then you regret it? Why? Don't say yes; don't say no. Say, 'I will think about it,' and then really put in the thought process to make sure you're going to make the right decision."

That statement changed my life. How many times have you said yes and been burnt and regretted it? How many times have you said no and felt like you should have said yes? You're entitled to think about decisions before you make them. Let yourself have this option so you can fully process all sides of any given situation, in sales or in your personal life.

8. Not Setting Viable Goals

Too often people aren't clear on their goals. Think through your goals and write them down. You need a physical reminder of where you are going, a roadmap to exactly where you want to be. When you begin externalizing your goals, prioritize them in steps so they are achievable. Then they will incrementally lead to fulfilling your dreams.

9. Not Being a Go-Getter

You might think not being a go-getter falls under a lack of confidence, but even the most confident people are not always ready to take that confidence to the next level. You can take all the business classes you want, get all the certifications possible, and still not excel in sales or your personal goals. Being a go-getter means taking it to the next level. It's more than just doing what everyone else is doing and doing it well. It means thinking outside of the box, coming up with new ideas, being innovative, and pushing the boundaries. It means overcoming obstacles by looking at a problem from a new perspective and then finding a solution. It means never giving up, no matter what, until you achieve your goal, and then, not resting on your laurels but going after the next big thing.

10. Unwillingness to Change

So far, this list might feel overwhelming because it may require you to change certain things. But just because you've always done something a certain way doesn't mean you can't change to get better results. The reality is that failure to change keeps you where you're at, but if you're willing to change from within, you can have the life you envision for yourself. Do it slowly and methodically. Be bold, vulnerable, and honest. When you change yourself, you become a better person, a better communicator, a better salesperson, and you build better relationships with people. Be good to yourself and remember that real change doesn't happen overnight.

If you feel unwilling to change, it's probably fear that is holding you back. Fear of the unknown is common. Some people dive right into a cold pool, while others dip their toes in just to test the waters, and it takes them half an hour before they really get in to swim. But why not dive in? So what if you feel a little chilly for a few minutes? What prevents people from diving in is fear of stepping outside their comfort zones—as I said, the fear of the unknown. If you want something bad enough, you have to jump in and not be afraid.

Focus on Today

The most beautiful part of my coaching business is sitting with another person and helping him identify the issues that imprison him. It's meaningful to watch people dig deep and turn their lives around.

I have a client who is married with four children. Every morning, by the time he would wake up, his wife had already prepared breakfast and shipped the kids off to school. She resented that he was not waking up earlier to be with the family or being more ambitious.

He had goals in his head, but, obviously, his time management skills were not properly prioritized. I asked him how he thought his relationship with his wife would change if he got up at 7:30 in the morning and helped her. I also asked him, "What if you got up earlier and began to work your plan and chip away at the goals you have written down?" We worked on a strategy to maximize extra time in the morning, and when he implemented it, this client went from earning $4,000 a month to well over $11,000 a month in a matter of seven months. This happened because this person committed to the change—he knew the water was cold and that he would feel uncomfortable, but he dove in anyway.

Thirty years ago, I met my mentor and he put a lot of time into me. I am not book smart, and I'm a knucklehead, but when I finally committed to the changes he asked of me, my income doubled, and then tripled. Let me tell you, if I can make these changes, like quitting smoking and developing personal skills, anyone can.

Remember, all this growth doesn't guarantee that every day will be a great day—it's a roller coaster out there—but you must stay positive and committed to these realizations. Someone once told me that if you keep a foot in yesterday and a foot in tomorrow, you're pissing away today. As crude as that is, it is very true; you must focus on today.

In your journey, don't try to be perfect. The day I'm perfect is when I'm six feet under. Living people cannot be perfect; instead, commit yourself to becoming a *better person* today and every day.

AUTHENTIC SELLING TIPS

1. Lack of confidence hinders personal and professional growth. Be willing to examine your life with honesty so you can gain the insights needed to develop the core fundamentals that will put dreams into action.

2. Survey your work habits in order to improve your business. Review my Top 10 "bad habits" list weekly.

3. Don't be impulsive. Feel empowered to say: "Let me think about it."

4. Don't fear the unknown. When new business ventures come into your life, have the core confidence and enterprising spirit to explore them.

5. Keep in mind that the concept of good communication skills doesn't just mean being an effective and articulate speaker; it also extends to being a good listener. Commit to improving your verbal *and* nonverbal communication.

FREEDOM QUESTIONS

1. What is your purpose? What do you most want to achieve that would make your life better?

_____

_____

_____

_____

_____

_____

2. What do you need to do to re-script your thoughts and your life so you can achieve that goal or purpose?

_____

_____

_____

_____

_____

_____

3. Where do you lack confidence in yourself and your abilities?

_____

_____

_____

_____

_____

_____

4. People gain confidence by becoming good at what initially feels uncomfortable. What can you do to gain confidence in the areas where it is lacking?

_____

_____

_____

_____

_____

5. Which of the ten bad habits listed in this chapter do you most need to work on? What will you commit to doing to change that bad habit?

_____

_____

_____

_____

_____

CHAPTER THREE
SINGING FOR A PRIZE

"THE HIGHEST PRIZE IN A WORLD OF MEN IS THE
MOST BEAUTIFUL WOMAN AVAILABLE ON YOUR ARM
AND LIVING THERE IN HER HEART LOYAL TO YOU."

— NORMAN MAILER

"You would have thought I was some famous singer in Las Vegas. It was surreal. It changed my life forever."

— *David Stern*

I n the 1990s, I spent a lot of time on the road alone, driving to different cities to give seminars on behalf of a company I represented based on the West Coast. I would drive to places like Boston and New Hampshire instead of flying because, believe it or not, traveling by car saved time. I wouldn't be dealing with airport bureaucracy.

For hours and hours, I would be sitting in the car, shooting the breeze with myself, barreling down the highway from one city to another.

Sometimes, the downtime was maddening; sometimes, it was thought-provoking; sometimes, it was a little bit of both. One particular time when it was a little bit of both, I started thinking of my favorite musical, *Fiddler on the Roof.* The soundtrack featured the wonderful song "If I Were A Rich Man." Mindlessly, I started singing the song like I had done so many times before.

As the road unfolded ahead of me, I started rewording the lyrics to amuse myself. Suddenly, the words "If

I *were a* rich man" became "If you *want to be a* rich man." *I'm onto something*, I thought to myself.

I started inserting different types of products and services I sold into the verses of the song, keeping my modified chorus refrain "If you *want to be a* rich man." It was clever and it passed the time.

Every three-hour drive was spent perfecting my little song. For months and months, I painstakingly redrafted this song. Finally, I had my masterpiece and I was excited to share it with my colleagues.

One time, I picked up my cellphone and called a counterpart of mine, Tom Carroll. He didn't pick up the phone, so I left a voicemail message and sang him the song. I was curious what he thought of it. Almost as soon as I finished the final verse, I forgot I had called him. It was just one of those fun impulsive moves.

Fast forward to that July. I was on my way to Toronto for an international sales convention. Over 1,700 people would attend. My job was to train attendees on company products and services in a session on Sunday.

Sunday morning arrived; I went up on stage and gave my presentation. In passing, I casually mentioned that the last time I came to Toronto, I had gone on a date. It was just a witty aside, but one woman in back was intrigued and asked one of our sales managers whether

I was single. He confirmed that I was, and they agreed to discuss this potential opportunity after the seminar.

My speaking portion lasted about an hour and thirty minutes. It went smoothly, and I neatly tied up the session. Then I walked offstage, feeling satisfied with my delivery. Right as I exited the stage, though, I heard Tom Carol say, "David, please come back; you're not done yet."

My heart dropped. I started going through the contour of the speech in my head. In an instant, I double-checked everything in my mind and concluded the speech was a success. What was he talking about? When I politely asked him, he shot back, "David, do you remember that song you sent me on voicemail?"

It was one of those moments when time stands still and you sort of have an out-of-body experience. Within seconds, I remembered leaving that message on Tom's voicemail during one of those epic sales journeys. I said, "Oh, my goodness. Yes." He responded, calmly, "Well, everybody here is waiting to hear the song."

I thought I was going to die. I'm not a singer, but now I was going to make my performance debut in front of 1,700 people! Not only was the audience beyond large, but it included company brass—the partners, vice presidents, and high ranking executives.

Tom said, "David, you have no choice. You have to do

this." I was scared, never having sung in public or to a group, but I said to myself, "David, you have nothing to lose. It's your moment for glory. Let's go. You are not a singer, but so what? Do what you've got to do."

The song was about the business. It was about the different products and services I had just talked about for an hour and a half. I told myself, "Blurt it out. What do you care?"

And before I knew it, everybody started clapping, so I took a deep breath and went through the song. Time again stood still, and everything was gone: the fear, the hesitation. You would have thought I was some famous singer in Las Vegas. It was surreal. It changed my life forever.

I thought the song was, at best, an inside joke between Tom and me. Truthfully, I didn't even think he would remember it a few days after my leaving it on his voicemail. It was just a silly gesture.

I had no idea that everyone in management already knew this song and, at the end of my presentation, they were already expecting me to sing it. I was totally clueless.

The aftermath of my impromptu performance was magical. Everybody came up to congratulate me, not only for the great seminar I gave, but for how I had created a great song that perfectly fit within the convention's context. Half an hour later, my manager introduced me to that woman I mentioned earlier. She would become the future Mrs. Stern.

I had already laid eyes on her Friday at registration. I was sitting around talking to people who wanted to learn more about the business and art of sales when I saw her. She was truly a vision. She stood there smoldering with dark, piercing eyes and radiant beauty. It was hard to concentrate on my sales small talk. Her sheer presence was magnetic.

I kept wondering, "Who is she?" So I struck up the nerve to go over to talk with her and introduce myself. We exchanged a few pleasantries, but we never got a chance to have a meaningful interaction, until I got offstage.

My wife remembers this a little differently (okay, quite a bit differently). I asked her to write her side of things because I figure she has the right to set the record straight. Please excuse this little sidetrack, but it will also somehow explain how this beautiful woman could be attracted to a guy like me. Without further ado, here is the incredible Judith Stern:

> *In the 1990s, while living in Israel, I joined a multi-level marketing organization that sold pre-paid phone cards. I came onboard thinking I would sell these American phone cards to physicians traveling to the U.S., and build a side business for myself.*

I had heard that the Vice President in charge of Sales was an Orthodox Jew (as am I) and if one wanted to learn to sell, one went to learn from the great "guru" himself, Mr. David Stern. Whatever he told you to do, it would be like the gospel and the Message from the Mount all wrapped in one.

After moving back to the States, I received a phone call from "the great one" himself, encouraging me to attend a sales convention in Toronto the following weekend. I was duly flattered and intimidated that the VP of Sales called me. It seemed rather farfetched that I would be able to attend. At the time, I was divorced and a single mother responsible for three kids. However, "the great guru" himself called several more times (he must have heard I was really awful at sales!), so I decided to attend at the last moment. (Thanks, Mom, for watching the kids.)

I drove as fast as I could from Detroit to Toronto so I wouldn't be late. I arrived at the hotel about four hours later and met the legendary David Stern in the flesh.

Needless to say, he wasn't what I expected. First of all, when I heard that he was a religious Jew, I pictured a beard, hat, and maybe even side-curls, but that wasn't what David Stern looked like. I met a rather short, heavyset, balding man with a smallish yarmulke and glasses. (By the way, wearing black

Dockers and white gym shoes—not a great look.) Though, he had a special twinkle in his eye, which gave the impression of someone very astute and intuitive, my first impression was that he seemed like "a real New York salesman." He had a kind of showmanship that struck me as rather insincere.

We sat and spoke for a while, after which I left to spend the Sabbath with a family I was visiting. I returned to the convention on Sunday morning to hear the speeches and attend the sales workshops.

After a number of rather unimpressive speakers, David Stern took to the stage. The first thing he said to a room of about 1,700 people (most of whom were not Jewish) was, "The last time I was in Toronto was for a Shidduch date" (a Yiddish term meaning he was set up on a blind date by a matchmaker). It was pretty funny to me, thinking how few people in the room actually knew what he meant, but he assumed they would all understand. My second thought was, "What? He's not married?!"

When I asked my colleague about that, I was told, "No, he is not married."

"Hmmm", I thought. "That's interesting." And I filed that little piece of information away.

David's speech was excellent, inspiring, and captivating. I was impressed. Then, before he left the stage, he sang a song to the tune of "If I Were a Rich Man" from Fiddler on the Roof, but he changed the words to: "I Want to Be A Rich Man," and sang about how one could become rich with this company. It was a hit, and I thought he was great. (I like a man with a good voice.)

Throughout the day, I attended sales workshops, and David would drop by the various meetings to help and advise. At the end of the day, all of the people who kept Kosher were going to a local Kosher restaurant for dinner, and I really wanted to be included. I didn't know at the time that David had told his people "make sure Judy goes."

I sat across from David at the restaurant (he ate chicken cacciatore), and I didn't eat much since I was still intimidated by the VP of Sales talking to me. We then went to another meeting in a private home. Before the meeting, David and I were in the room before the others joined us, and he said the first really personal thing to me: "You know," he said, "I need to lose fifty pounds." I had mentioned to him that I had been a personal trainer at one time, and I suspect that's why he made that comment. But, oh boy, what was I supposed to say to that? So I offered to give him a fitness program. A little later, I snuck out of the meeting and drove back to Detroit.

A few weeks later, David called again to tell me he

would be in Detroit for a sales meeting, and he asked if I could pick him up from the airport. I wasn't able to, but I met him at the meeting, and a group of us went to the Kosher restaurant in town, where my mother met us with my kids. (She was introduced to David at that point.) So when David asked if I could drive him back to the airport, my mother agreed to watch the kids. We talked some more during that drive, and I heard some of David's life story. I dropped him off, and that was that.

When I got home, he called, told me that his flight was delayed, and we ended up talking for about three hours. We have been talking ever since. We were married in 2001, and we are still convinced that the reason that phone card company came into existence was so we could meet. God works in mysterious ways.

This is why sales are so significant in life. We are always "selling" ourselves, whether we realize it or not. I know because I bought the "whole package."

Regards from one very happy customer.

I look back incredulously at that journey, from the long car rides, to playfully rewriting "If I Were A Rich Man," to my appearance at that Toronto sales convention, to wonderfully concluding with meeting my wife. What if I had done things differently?

At the beginning of my career, I had a colleague I would travel with who always offered me advice on public speaking. He once said to me, "David, one day you are going to be speaking in front of thousands of people." I told him I thought he was crazy.

The funny thing is, not too many years later, I wound up at the Mirage Hotel in Las Vegas, speaking in front of a few thousand people. I was sick to my stomach doing it. But I did it. Then I started to get used to it. I became able to do it.

As nervous as I was and as scared as I was, I felt so good about speaking in public because I knew I had the future in front of me and I could go anywhere and build anything—any business—for people all over the world. My confidence was there.

How many of you out there have had similar experiences, or felt there was something inside you that you were meant to do, but you couldn't externalize it? How many of you have dreams, aspirations, or goals that you have to hold back because of the status of your current professional life? Having fear, lack of confidence, or lack of self-worth is what truly holds you back. Everyone has a song to sing.

Willingness to Change

That glorious life-changing moment I've shared with

you speaks to one profound aspect of our everyday existence: the willingness to make changes.

We all are shackled to fears, the past, toxic thinking, unhealthy relationships, and negative mindsets. These things don't go away—they eat at you until they devour your heart and your spirit. Nothing changes until *you* make the changes.

How do you free yourself from these defeating and unnecessary forces in your life? By looking in the mirror and facing them, and then having the courage to strategize for a better future with a tangible and accountable plan of action.

The first step is to identify your goals. I'm not talking about goals in your head, because I know, for me, I have a lot of junk between my two ears. There's only a certain amount of gigabytes of memory that I can tap into in my brain. What are your goals on paper? If you have goals on paper, if there's anything in the world that you want and you're seriously honest about it, there's no way in the world that you can get there without having a roadmap. If you don't already have your goals on paper, put them down.

Once you get that done, take it one step further. Hang them up on the wall. Now, you've got it in beautiful black letters all over your apartment or your office— your roadmap to your future destination.

Next, it's all about taking action. It's what you do on a daily basis that will help you realize your dreams. For people in sales, action means rigorous database management. Every day, you should be building bridges to closing deals by establishing new prospects and staying in touch with current clients and prospects. Cold calling and knocking on doors is difficult, but each day you have to push through.

To maximize your effectiveness, prioritize what you need to do. Having an organized to-do list or plan of action is going to help you get to where you want to go. It takes patience, dedication, and hard work to map out a journey.

Stay focused despite the distractions inherent in the business of sales. I know for me, as a salesperson, if I'm hanging out with a friend of mine for lunch and we're going to have a quick bite to eat, we'll schmooze for a little bit. If we take forty-five minutes and we turn it into an hour and a half, that's not goal-oriented. Now we're taking time away from our mission. Now, we're doing something against our goals. It's not going to help us get to where we want to go.

That said, at times, you need to refuel and get away from the hustle. Maybe you go out and play nine holes of golf. You have to have that breathing space, but the next day you need to get back on target. The message here is to think strategically and purposefully about your downtime; make it work for you as a resting point after a lot of heavy work.

Achieving Independence

In my practice over the last five years, I have worked with people, whether one-on-one or in groups, to help each person individually grow and develop according to the best of his or her ability and skill sets. For me, that is the most beautiful thing in the world.

If I can help you achieve your goal, whether it is putting money away for your child's college education, putting money away for your child's wedding, putting money away into your 401K, or even, more importantly, getting out of debt, then I have achieved my goal. If I can help make one person's family happy, I am a success.

Now, I'm not going to help you unless you can first help yourself. I'm not going to cold call for you. I'm not going to knock on doors for you. I'm not going to call to make appointments for you. I can guide you in how to do this work effectively, but what I teach is independence.

Isn't that what you want? Isn't that what you're looking for? Freedom? That's my job. There's nothing I'd rather do than teach you how to achieve your goals and dreams, whether you're earning $50,000 and want to make $150,000, or you're earning $250,000 and want to take a company to $50 million in sales. There's a personal satisfaction in helping another human being.

I want to be clear that I'm not special. I am no different than any single one of you. I just have more years of experience from the bumps of the roller coaster. I've done it many times. I might go through it today. Who cares? I'm constantly moving forward because if I'm not moving forward, chances are I'm going to go backwards, and no one wants to go backwards.

I have a fresh vision of you, for you. Often, salespeople lose perspective in lean times. Their self-esteem suffers, they sleep late, their ambition drops, and then their lives begin to unravel. But this cycle doesn't have to happen, even when times are bad.

Sometimes the foundation or the beginning of a new life of opportunity begins because of one simple thing: being excited to wake up in the morning. Instead of dulling the senses with late television, you turn in early to be fresh for the day.

Nothing feels better than waking up to explore fresh and exciting opportunities. Having promising appointments buoys the soul. You go to bed feeling thankful, and you bounce out of bed feeling inspired. That energy makes more energy, and pretty soon, you're drastically increasing your business.

I would love for you to be excited to get up even if it's

raining. After all, it's going to rain. Who cares? When it's really beautiful out there, all of the salespeople are out there (including your competitors). But when it's raining, sleeting, and hailing, there's nobody out there. That's the best opportunity. So it's raining. So it's snowing. So what? The customer is ready to see you.

You need to live today like it is the best or most important day of your life. Make the best of it. And then the next morning, wake up and be grateful that you have another day to take a shot at it. Then, at night, you can take the whole day, put it aside, and feel satisfied that you had a great day. Maybe you didn't make any sales, but you went out and did what you had to do, and for that, you can always feel grateful.

Gratitude and hard work bring success. It's not about being greedy or cutthroat; it's about being humble and hardworking. The world doesn't revolve around me. I can listen to other people, listen to my wife, listen to the kids, and see what's going on with them. It's all about them.

If you can envision a life like this, and it's not far-fetched, you're going to be the happiest person in the world. I'm the happiest person in the world today. I might not have the most money, but guess what? I'm living a very healthy, good life today. That's what I wish for all my clients. Isn't that what you want?

Forward Movement

Have you ever tried to cross a path with a puddle smack in the middle of it? It's frustrating and makes you anxious. We may even panic a little and stare at the puddle. We don't want to get wet because maybe we just polished our shoes and have on a fresh ironed pair of pants. But what do you think is going to happen if you're just standing there gazing at that puddle? Absolutely nothing—if there isn't any forward movement.

You either have to go around that puddle, jump over it hoping you can make it, or do something right away because otherwise you're just wasting time. This image is a metaphor for change.

What are you resisting change for? What's the worst thing that's going to happen? You might get a little splash of water because your heel is going to hit the water and you're going to splash your pants. So what? What's the big deal? It's only water. Eventually, it is going to dry.

Resisting change is not going to help you get to where you want to go. It will keep you stuck in a lack of confidence. Why do you want to stay stuck? I'm not asking you to make big changes; big changes are hard to make and they don't always stick. But if you chip away slowly but surely, you're going to get there.

Have you ever tried to have a drink that's ice cold, and all of a sudden, you get brain freeze? After that jolt of cold, you quickly figure out that smaller sips make the temperature more manageable. Before you know it, you have found a way to truly enjoy that bottle of beer or soda pop. Approach change like you would an ice cold drink; take small sips, and eventually, you will get to finish your drink.

In 1985, my mentor said something unforgettable, "David, the only person who is going to help you change your life is you. That person you see in the mirror in the morning when you brush your teeth, that's the guy who can lift you up or drag you down."

Another thing my mentor told me is that when you point your finger at someone else, it is because *you* lack confidence. When I suffered from procrastination or other issues, I often pointed my finger at someone else. It's always easier to blame someone else.

There was a time when I was stuck in a funk. I made money, but I wanted to make more, and I couldn't break through the financial ceiling. I blamed the company, I blamed the product, and I blamed everyone else. Every time I would rant about my frustration with the state of my life, my mentor would tell me, "David, when you point the finger at someone else, there's always three little fingers that point right back at you. Before you blame someone else, look at yourself three times and ask, 'What's my role in this?' Look in the mirror. That's the person who is going to help you."

That advice liberated me and helped me break through my career and financial holdbacks. I was being resistant; it took some time, but slowly, I realized the benefit of breaking out of my self-imposed cell or prison.

Take a few minutes right now and look in that mirror. You have the power to change.

No Detours

I have spent a lot of time—years—on the road traveling. When you drive from one town to the next or one city to the next, there is a lot of time for daydreaming. However, instead of daydreaming, think about your goals, then put them down in writing, and spend your time achieving those goals. I usually carry a small recorder with me to take notes of ideas. When I get home, I listen to the recorder, write down the good stuff, and toss out the rest.

I have a client in Michigan who is always telling me, "I'm going to have a house in Palm Springs. I'm going to have a beach house in Miami and Hawaii, and I'm going to have all these homes. BLAH, BLAH, BLAH." This guy is in la-la land. I say, "Excuse me; what are you doing to get these houses?" Dreaming big is wonderful, but it's all just fantasy—smoke and mirrors—until you actually commit to doing the work through actionable steps.

In 1978, I got a brand new car, so I was excited to drive cross-country to California to begin a new job and what felt like a new life. We didn't have GPS at the time. So in order to get to California, I had to have a map. Sometimes, it was a few maps to get me from key points in my journey to other key points. This experience sticks out in my mind as a beautiful metaphor for big goals and dreams being reached through a number of smaller milestones.

One thing you have to remember is that travel is rarely direct. Maybe a main travel artery is closed for maintenance or because of a natural disaster. Now you have a detour. You need to consult your map to consider the full range of options available to you to move forward.

Now, besides a good roadmap with flexible options, the rubber has to hit the pavement. I have to put the car in drive. To clarify the metaphor here, you have to make sure you move forward each day, no matter what the detours are.

Daydream all you want, but if you actually want to arrive at your destination, you need to hit the road; you need to have a map, or two, and be able to maintain your course despite the detours.

Enjoy the Ride

All journeys take time, so remember, things are not

going to change overnight. It takes some work, it takes some effort, and it takes some doing. Some of you might be twenty-two years old, and some of you are forty-five or even sixty years old. You didn't get where you are overnight. You got there by whatever it took you to get there. It's going to take some time to do this.

I was thirty-one when I started working under my mentor. At the time, I'd had some success, but I wanted to uplift my career and my earnings. I was fidgety from wanting to get there fast—to make that quick buck.

During this profound time, I sensed that change would mean personal development. Intuitively, I knew this was the route, but it took me a lot of time to wrap my head around how gradual the changes would be. You can't drive from California to New York in one day. I needed to be patient and proactive.

It is important to mention that I did not go to an Ivy League school or any college. I barely passed high school. But I guarantee you this: if hard-headed me can make profound changes in my life, so can you. All you need is to be focused, have patience, perseverance, and a clear grasp of T.I.M.E. (Things I Must Earn).

Along the way, be kind to yourself. We make mistakes; we screw things up. So what? We try, and it takes time to improve and change. It took me a long time to get to where I am today. As difficult and painful as it might be with the ups and downs and the roller coasters you will ride, you will look back and see how wonderful of a trip it was.

I changed my life. I became a better person, and I earned more money. I went from one income level to another, to the next, to the next. Looking back from where I am right now to where I came from, it's nothing but beautiful. Isn't that something you want?

Whatever ideas you have, whatever issues you have, there are steps to take to transform your life into just what you envision. You need to undertake this new adventure gradually. If you don't go up to the first step, you can't get to step two. If you don't go up to step two, you can't get to step three. Your goals and your plan of action are written in an order because that order makes sense, and by reaching your goals one step at a time, you can take a lot of pressure off yourself and prevent frustration from thinking, "I can't do this."

Let me give you a little analogy here. You fly overseas or fly from the East Coast to the West Coast or vice versa. Your plane takes off and it's a beautiful day, but then you hear the pilot say, "We're going to be running into a storm." You know that sooner or later you're going to get out of that storm. You're going to get out of that mess, and you're going to be back into clarity. You're going to be back into beautiful clear skies, smooth sailing. You know it's going to be an hour, two hours, maybe three hours, depending on the type of trip. It's going to happen. You will get through the storm and land safely.

What I'm here to tell you is that all these obstacles are like living in a cloud. You can't see, and you don't know where the wall, door, or window is. You can't feel anything because you're living in such a haze. But once the fog lifts, you're going to be able to get into a life of clarity if you use these steps to get out and get back into life and enjoy the ride.

Roller coasters are phenomenal. You go up, you go down, there are twists and turns, and everything else is part of the process. It's part of the fun, and it's part of the excitement. But once you have more clarity, it makes a big difference. Would you want to go on the roller coaster when it's raining or storming? I don't think so. But when it's a nice, clear, beautiful day, you don't care how many twists, turns, and flips it makes. You're having a great time. You know what? Get out of the fog you're in. Get out of the prison you've created for yourself and get on the roller coaster ride. Every single day, make it happen. Take this information, use it to move forward, and make your goals happen for yourself so you'll always be on a beautiful roller coaster ride.

You might say, "No, we're in sales; we go up, and we go down." Yes, but you don't have to go down so deep and stay stuck. You don't have to repeat the same mistakes over and over again. Albert Einstein said once that the definition of insanity is repeating the same mistakes over and over again and expecting different results. Well, if we want to stay and do the same things we're doing, we're going to get the same results. We expect different results with nothing different.

Keep It Simple

Some of you might think changing is complicated, but it really isn't. You take baby steps. When you were a baby, you crawled before you were able to stand or walk; you couldn't run. How many times before you got to stand and walk did you fall? You did get up again, and you fell again. Sometimes, you bumped your head, you cried, and Mom put a Band-Aid on you, but you crawled quite a bit before you stood up.

The same thing happens when you learn to ride a bike. Dad is holding on to your bicycle to make sure you don't fall. You have training wheels to make sure you stay balanced, and you still have a helping hand. To become an expert in sales, you crawl, you fall, but you get up and continue until you make it. Find a good coach or mentor to be your training wheels until you're ready to ride on your own. You'll know when you're ready.

This book is about identifying where you are at, where you want to be, and how to make the trip from the present to the future. It's all very simple. Keep it simple.

AUTHENTIC SELLING TIPS

1. We all have a song to sing. Be bold and sing it—that moment of taking a chance could alter the course of your life.

2. Don't let resistance because of panic or frustration prevent you from moving forward.

3. Make a roadmap to your dreams and each day make sure your travel forward, no matter what.

FREEDOM QUESTIONS

1. What is your favorite upbeat, positive song? Some examples might be "Somewhere Over the Rainbow," "Don't Rain on My Parade," or "To Dream the Impossible Dream." Write the title below. Then rewrite the lyrics to support your dream. Use a piece of paper if you need more space.

_____

_____

_____

_____

_____

_____

_____

_____

_____

_____

_____

_____

_____

_____

_____

_____

_____

_____

_____

2. List ten things in your life for which you feel grateful. Whenever you feel tempted to focus on what's wrong in your life, pull out this list to change your mindset.

1. _____

2. _____

3. _____

4. _____

5. _____

6. _____

7. _____

8. _____

9. _____

10. _____

3. What do you tend to blame for blocking you from pursuing your goals? What role are you playing that allows this situation to continue? How can you play a different role?

_____

_____

_____

_____

_____

_____

_____

_____

_____

_____

_____

4. Create a map for where you want to go. List the steps that will get you to your destination:

Step 1: _____

Step 2: _____

Step 3: _____

Step 4: _____

Step 5: _____

Final Destination: _____

CHAPTER FOUR
SHARPENING YOUR AXE

"Give me six hours to chop down a tree and I will spend the first four sharpening the axe."

— Abraham Lincoln

"Are you ready? This is going to be a workout."

— David Stern

I hope you've been enjoying my personal stories. My goal with them has been to use my own personal journey to enlighten and inspire you in an entertaining fashion. I want to show you how personal development is intrinsically tied to becoming a better salesperson. In this chapter, however, I want to give you ten laser-focused insights from my four decades in the business of sales. Are you ready? This is going to be a workout.

We will start with a few linked fundamentals to the business of sales: time management, database management, prospecting, and product knowledge. I was not always an expert at these skills; I, too, had to learn them along my journey.

The first time I was *really* out there selling was when I was in the jewelry business in California. I had to go from store to store, town to town, city to city, state to state. That was my first experience of *real* selling. When I worked in the bank, I was sitting in one place and people were coming and going—doing their own thing. I was just sitting there, waiting, and being responsive to someone coming up to my window or my desk. Going out and selling in the jewelry business was my first challenge.

I was fortunate enough that the person who had the line for fifteen years before me, and who had created this West Coast territory, was willing to teach me a thing or two about the way I should be running my business.

He taught me that it was important to focus on time management, database management, and to prospect constantly for new potential customers. If I were in a certain city or town, where I already have a customer or two, I should always look around or do my homework in advance to find out how many other possible jewelry stores were in the neighborhood or surrounding area. He always added, "Never forget success in sales comes from building relationships."

He also taught me that product knowledge was very important. I knew nothing about jewelry. I had never owned a bangle, a bracelet, or a ring. I had never had anything like that in my life. I had trays and trays of jewelry I was supposed to sell, but I didn't know anything about any of it. At first, it was okay to learn the product on the job, by letting the customer teach you, but after some time, you needed to make sure you became an expert.

Shrimp Earrings

My very first client was in Beverly Hills. Her name was Mrs. Lewis, of Beverly Hills Jewelers. I called her up to make my first appointment, and I introduced myself to her. "My name is David Stern, and I'm replacing Lou Hirsch. I'd like to come and show you my wares and introduce myself." She replied, "It's good to hear from you, and I'm looking forward to meeting you. By the way, David, do you have shrimp earrings?"

Shrimp earrings? I was quietly thinking, *I don't know what shrimp earrings are!* All I knew was that I had seventeen trays of earrings. I said, "Mrs. Lewis, I have seventeen trays of earrings. I'm sure you will be able to pinpoint what you need. When can we meet?" She gave me an appointment for twelve o'clock, a day or two later.

I was nervous. This was my first call in the jewelry business. I was dressed in a suit and tie, rolling my big suitcases on wheels, coming into this jewelry store with a smile on my face, but I was nervous as hell on the inside. After I gave her my card, she said, "Come into my conference room; have a seat." After some chit chat, she said, "Okay, Mr. Stern; can you show me your earrings?" I took out seventeen trays of earrings and she went through the first tray, second tray, third tray, and fourth tray. I was dripping with sweat as she continued looking for shrimp earrings. All of a sudden, she pointed and said, "Aha! This is what I'm looking for."

I discovered I had four or five different sizes of shrimp earrings. I had learned about my product on the job. Then she said, "You're here. You might as well let me look at your chains." Soon, I had learned about serpentine chains. I learned about herringbone chains. I learned about the different styles of bangles, bracelets, rings, and all that kind of stuff. This lady unknowingly helped me, and I took notes to understand what she was talking about, so the next time I went to a client, I would have some knowledge.

By allowing myself to be teachable and letting others show me what I didn't know, I immensely helped my career. Eventually, I started to develop a profile in the jewelry business. People would call me up and say, "David, what's selling in Southern California? Beverly Hills? What are they selling nowadays?" And you know what I would say? "Shrimp earrings, serpentine chains, and herringbone chains." I became the biggest seller of shrimp earrings and herringbone chains. Why? Because that's what my customer in Beverly Hills bought, so I thought that was what everybody would buy. Everybody started buying them, and they were selling the hell out of them. Those were great days.

No's and Yes's

During this period of my life, I was learning the value of time management and database management. My territory included Los Angeles and every town and city from Bakersfield, California, to Seattle, Washington, including Hawaii. I covered the entire area every six weeks even during the brutally hot summer seasons.

My routine included dropping in on stores, introducing myself, and then trying to show the store clerks my line. Often, they would say, "Well, you know, why don't you come back some other time because we're not interested right now. It's the slow season. We'll look at this again later." I would say, "Oh, sure, no problem," and leave my card.

It felt like everyone was saying the same thing in the summer because consumers don't really go out to buy jewelry in that unpleasant hot season. At times, it was so hot in the summer that by 11 a.m., I couldn't wait for 6 p.m. to get to my hotel and down a few ice cold beers. There was no other marketplace incentive during those months, such as Christmas or Easter, so I got all these "No's."

Being turned away constantly started to chip away at my confidence. In the summer season, I did well in the big city areas of Beverly Hills, Los Angeles, and San Francisco, but the inland route from Bakersfield and north was impenetrable. I went from making thousands of dollars in commission to lows and "No's."

When the weather finally started to cool down, I became better at understanding time management, database management, and prospecting. I started becoming more methodical in my route, streamlining time spent with clients and time spent between meeting clients. I became more diligent with maintaining my database and hunting down leads.

I started making sure I could see as many people as possible, and I went on each client visit feeling purposeful, optimistic, and confident. All of a sudden, people started to say yes. In sales, "No" is the path to get to "Yes."

The Rhythm of the Market

Over the five or six years I worked in the jewelry business, I noted the rhythm of the market. Summer was always slow, but in the fall, I needed to be vigilant with sales basics like follow-up, time management, database management, and prospecting.

Come summertime, I would plan ahead for fall by prospecting, making tons of follow-up calls, and doing database management. This meant I would continue working my usual route and maybe try to meet some new clients, but I knew in my head no one was really going to buy. I was simply laying down foundations for future sales. Maintaining face-to-face contact kept me in the game and built stronger bonds with my customers because when clients are going to get ready to buy, they'll buy from the person who came in when they didn't need him. That was me.

Good database management means knowing prospect lists, client lists, and the bases you're going to touch on the road. When I was in the jewelry business, I would drive from L.A. to Las Vegas, San Francisco, Portland, and Seattle, all of which were part of my territory. Effective time management included planning my trip departures and appointments ahead of time, knowing what road I wanted to take, whom exactly I would visit, and, if I had enough time, fitting in some new prospect visits. You constantly have to visit clients and prospect for new ones. You never know when an old customer is going to leave you, or when a company is going to go out of business, so you always have to prospect.

Now, whether people would buy or not, I didn't know. That was the unknown. I couldn't be sure what the outcome of a customer or prospect visit would be. The only thing I knew for certain was that customers definitely weren't going to buy if I didn't show up.

The key to making things happen is to make phone calls and appointments, and to be physically out there saying hello to the clients or prospects. Take the car, go to your client, say hello, shake a hand, and go back on the road. Take your show on the road. That's what it takes. You have to get out there.

Knowing the Benefits

We touched on product knowledge a little bit with the story of the shrimp earrings. In that instance, I got away with learning on the job and kind of faking it. But a lot of sales nowadays are technology-based. We are living in something of a gadget/computer-based revolution. Now, thorough product knowledge is essential.

When I was working for Motorola, I had to understand every aspect of the products I was representing. That included the technology, features, and *benefits* of each. Yes, *benefits*. People don't buy features; they buy *benefits*.

In 1986, cellphone technology was brand new. Service was not available in every little nook and cranny in this country. You could travel sometimes for hours without having service.

One thing I quickly learned from the cellphone business was that it was important for me to be finding out my client's particular needs. For example, if I were sitting with an executive who commuted daily from Greenwich to New York City, I would inquire about productivity during travel time, etc. What were the client's hot buttons?

Often, these commuting executives were losing valuable time, and they didn't even know it! My line of questioning would be about how they would better like to use the time. How could they make the dead time between Greenwich and New York more productive? In this instance, the benefits of owning a cellphone are checking in at the office, having phone meetings, making deals, and calling their husbands or wives to let them know their schedule.

For commuters who travel by car, I would explore the safety route. The benefits of a cellphone for these people were being able to call AAA and to dial 911 in an emergency. In this instance, a cellphone's benefits were almost lifesaving!

By asking benefit questions, you're showing that you know your product. You understand not only what it does, but also how it can improve the lives of your clients and customers.

The Sales Essentials

In this section, I'd like to drill down hard on the business of sales essentials. This Top 10 list applies to everyone. For newbies, these basics are the fundamentals for building a thriving sales career. For pros, not only is this a good kick in the butt refresher course, but reviewing this list might also engage you in a fresh way and spark some growth and change in your sales approach. First the full list, and then I'll give you an explanation of each item. Let's get rolling….

TOP TEN SALES ESSENTIALS

1. Communication

2. Customer Service

3. Interpersonal Skills

4. Empathy Skills

5. Goals

6. Negotiation Skills

7. Decision Making

8. Referrals

9. Creativity

10. Innovation

1. Communication

How do you communicate with other people? What is your own self-perception? Outsiders can easily see and feel how we perceive ourselves. Some of us can see ourselves as pioneering, competitive, confident, and everything else. What happens, though, when we're stressed out? What happens when things don't go well? What happens if we just lost an account? What happens if we just lost a large commission? Our self-perception changes, and that's quickly telegraphed to other people. Other people can see that something is not right because we're not the same friendly, outgoing, positive, confident person. We become something else. We can be demanding, opinionated, and aggressive, and people can be offended by our negativity. Learning how to communicate better with other people is an extremely important skill.

First of all, adjust the way you are. For example, just because you had a bad experience with a client—you just lost a client, you lost a commission, a sale got cancelled—and you're upset, you cannot show it to your next customer; you need to make sure you are effectively communicating with that person, without him seeing that you're troubled about something. Being self-aware of how you feel and how you present yourself is crucial. When you meet a client, you want to know how the client is doing, not let on how you are doing.

To succeed at good communication, you must demonstrate interest in others. Treat them with respect, courtesy, and consideration. Listen well to them. When we're stressed, we tend to listen to the chaos in our heads, not to the clients.

In order to communicate effectively, it is extremely important to develop and maintain relationships with different kinds of people. It doesn't make a difference who you meet, who they are, or what sex, color, race, or religion they are; being able to communicate effectively transcends all differences.

2. Customer Service

In sales, I find that I have different issues when it comes to customer service with different companies. Many times, companies have a customer service department, so the client knows he can call there. Other times, clients see us, the salesperson, as the customer service. So, let's say someone got a bad shipment or a wrong shipment; he calls us, the salesperson, right away, even if the company has a robust customer service department. In this instance, we have to be involved and show that we're involved. It's our job to be the liaison between the customer and customer service.

I'm not just here to sell to people; I'm here to service them as well. Many other salespeople are only interested in selling, selling, selling, and many of those people are extremely selfish. They care about themselves, and they don't care about the client. I care about the client all the way so I can make sure he or she is satisfied.

When customer service calls me to say a problem is solved, I will call the customer to make sure everything was completed to his satisfaction. By doing this, the customer sees how involved I am, even though it was a customer service issue. Give customers a good feeling and they will think: *This person is a good salesperson.* If you are a good salesperson by taking care of the customer, he is going to want to remain your customer. What are the chances then that customers will give you referrals if you ask for them? So it's not just for the short-term; it's for the long-term because when they need something, they're going to call on you since they know you're reliable. You're not going to take their money and run.

3. Interpersonal Skills

Interpersonal skills are all about building rapport and relating well to all kinds of people, as we talked about before when discussing communication. One way to strengthen interpersonal skills is to focus on the clients. Make your interactions all about them. Ask them about themselves, how they're doing, and what their needs are. That makes people feel good, and it paves the way toward client and salesperson trust.

How do you let someone know that you understand him? By listening and asking questions. When you're trying to gain knowledge of a particular area and people are telling you something, and you ask them questions about it, they feel you care and understand them. People will know that you're listening and paying attention, and they're going to feed you the information you need. One thing I would suggest that you always try to do is to clarify what the person just said. That's an extremely important skill and, depending on what you're selling, it can be crucial in selling to a client through the product-benefits approach we discussed earlier.

4. Empathy Skills

Unfortunately, a lot of hardcore salespeople drive hard bargains above everything else, and they make a lot of money doing it. Are they very well-liked by people? Sometimes, but many times, no. Will people buy from them over and over again? Probably not. A sale is not about selling just for money. Personally, I care about other people. I have concerns. I respect other people. I'm not just taking their money. You have to have respect for them. You have to care about them. Be sensitive to people's emotions and experiences.

If I have a client that I want to have for many years, I'm going to do everything I can to get to know this person and to care about him. What you need to do is empathize with your clients; realize that they have their own businesses, their own families—they are not just a part of your own bottom line. By empathizing with your clients, they will see that you have concern and respect for them, which will ultimately improve your relationship. Empathy—or being able to understand, identify, and care about others—is another important interpersonal skill you should practice.

5. Goals

We talked earlier about setting tangible goals, just like driving cross-country from New York to California. But deciding to drive to California is simply not enough; you have to be more specific. Where in California? Why do you need to go there? You cannot achieve your goals if you don't have a clear image in mind before you embark.

To make a great living in sales, you have to have goals. You make your bottom line to do the work, but maybe you also have to feed a family or you want to buy a really nice house. You have to have S.M.A.R.T. goals to pay for these things. S.M.A.R.T. stands for goals that are specific, measurable, attainable, realistic, and timely.

You have to be mobile, active, and doing something in order to achieve your goals. You have to spend the time and effort to achieve the goal. You have to recognize and understand the opportunities available and work accordingly every single day to achieve your goals because, as salespeople, a lot of time wasters can get in our way. We waste a lot of time daydreaming, having long lunches, or procrastinating. The reason we don't achieve our goals may be because of these time wasters or other issues that won't allow us to stay focused.

Let me tell you how to become goal-oriented. I have this program called "Climb the Ladder to Success." It uses the ladder metaphor to explain how we make progress in anything we do. For example, if you are going to change some shingles on top of the roof of your house, you're going to put up a ladder to climb up there. You're going to make sure you have a good, strong ladder, not one bent out of shape, and when you lean it up against the house, you're going to make sure its angle is right and it has a strong foundation. You're not going to let it stand crooked; you're going to make sure it's straight, and that the foundation is flat and hard, not a soft muddy ground. You check all these things because if that ladder moves an inch when you're climbing it, you're dead.

To climb the ladder of success, you also need a solid foundation; you've got the product knowledge, you've got your goal orientation, you want to go up there, you have your database management, and you know exactly what you need to do, so now you're going to go step by step until you get to the top. You're not going to go two steps at a time because then you might slip and break your neck. You're not going to carry too much weight because you're going to slip. So what you're going to do is steadily climb each step, one at a time. You're going to go up until you get to the top.

In my "Climb the Ladder to Success" program, the first step is to know what you need on a monthly basis. What are your operating expenses? What's your budget? How much are you spending on gas, electric, telephone, utilities, mortgage or rent, car payments—

whatever it is. Let's say it's $5,000. That means you have to earn a minimum of $5,000 a month to complete the first step. Now you also have to consider taxes, depending on how you work and whom you work for. If you are on commission, it could be a 1099 or it could be a W2. You have to figure that in; that's the first step.

My second step is creating another goal. So what that means is, let's say for instance, you earn $5,000. That's what you need for your budget. Now what happens if you make $6,000? Then you have an extra $1,000. Where is that money going to? There has to be a goal. Well, maybe it's going to sit in the savings account. Maybe it's going to fill in a reserve account because we should all have nine, ten, or twelve months of reserve money just in case something happens. The third step is to make another incremental goal. This way, you slowly climb the ladder to success, step by step, but it's all goal-oriented; you need to be focused on those goals and have the commitment. If you're not committed to it, chances are you're not going to succeed. You have to commit to it.

6. Negotiation Skills

Negotiation is the process of working with a buyer or a company to reach an agreement on pricing or billing. To negotiate a deal, you need to understand that everyone wants to get something out of it. I'm the seller, you're the buyer, so I'm trying to sell, you're trying to buy, but we've got to negotiate the price or the service, whatever it is. To be a good negotiator, you have to be able to listen, identify, and understand what the other party wants. It comes back to interpersonal skills. If you don't build that skill, chances are you're not going to be able to negotiate very well.

If you communicate well, you understand the person you are negotiating with, and he knows that you understand him so he will do business with you. It's all part and parcel of a good communications skill set. Now most salespeople don't have the negotiation skill set well-developed. When I worked at Motorola, at some point in negotiating a big deal, I needed to involve upper management to negotiate. My job was to introduce a product, introduce the service, introduce the price, and give a basic underpinning of what the sale was about, but once it became more technical, I had to bring in technical people, and sometimes, financial people, in order to negotiate the deal. A deal should be for both parties; they should all agree. In that, there is a little give and take.

I wasn't a big negotiator. I allowed other people to come and do the negotiation. So don't think that just because you're in sales, you have to be the best negotiator. There are people who are very well-equipped in the skill of negotiation, but if I understand what the person needs, then I can communicate to upper management what this person is thinking or feeling or whatever the case might be. That way, upper management has a pretty good understanding of this person coming into the meeting. A negotiator also needs communication skills and then he can take it from there. So with negotiation, most salespeople don't have to be the best negotiators unless they're business owners, but that's a whole different ball game.

7. Decision Making

There's one thing I have to make clear. I cannot make a decision for my client. My clients make the decisions for themselves. I have to make decisions for myself, too.

As a salesperson, you decide for yourself whether or not you have a worthwhile customer. You decide for yourself whether it is worth your time to go there.

When deciding to represent a specific company, vet the entire opportunity. You need to investigate the service, product, and the people behind the company. It's very important to consider the people at any given company before you decide to work there. Consider their demeanor, communication skills, interpersonal skills, the company's public face/public perception, the spirit in the office, and how well they treat their employees. In this last instance, investigate employee satisfaction and turnover rate. You do this simply by talking to employees or other people, simply by asking around.

Now, once you make a decision, get off your butt and do something about it.

8. Referrals

The beauty of selling is being able to come back to existing customers to grow your clientele. To do that, keep people happy after the sale. It could mean coming back to a person to show him new features on his product, or just checking in with regard to customer satisfaction with a previously purchased product. In both instances, you're building better relationships. Service like this makes that person exclaim, "Wow, this salesperson is really good!" Then he refers you to other customers.

To get referrals, you need to learn continuously about the products and services you represent, and to follow up and demonstrate to your clients that you care, even when a deal is not pending. This all leads to referrals, and that's how you build a client base.

9. Creativity

In sales, you can become very creative. How do I overcome an objection? How do I talk to people differently? How do I manage my territory better? How do I manage my sales communication better? You become creative to deal with these obstacles.

Artists don't come to their work fully formed; they become creative over time. When you do things over and over again, you get better and better at them. The first couple of pictures artists paint are probably not so nice looking. They take a bunch of crayons and just scribble. But as you get older, as you get more into sales and learn more about it, as you continuously learn the art of selling, you become more creative. You discover how to approach people, a prospect or client. You create an approach that allows you to relate to your customers—maybe you weave in some personal stories to establish warmth and humility with them.

Nobody is born being creative. You work on it over time. Edison took a while to create his masterpieces. It took him 10,000 tries before he created the lightbulb. Get creative.

10. Innovation

When I worked for Motorola, I would park my car in a parking lot before I saw each client. The downtime helped me gather my thoughts and brainstorm ways to grow my business. Sometimes, I would see livery drivers and limousine drivers sitting in their cars, too.

I would hand them my card—maybe they could use a cellphone—and then notice that they would use my business card to pick their teeth, like a toothpick. So I got a bunch of toothpicks, and each time I gave a card to a driver, I included a toothpick.

It was a joke, but guess what? This joke turned into a lot of money. People were so excited about those toothpicks that , eventually, they wound up calling me. They didn't forget this incident. They said, "Mr. Stern, I met you in this parking lot. You gave me a toothpick." It was funny. It was innovative because I was giving them a little helpful trinket and a business card. It was a memorable and unique gesture that stirred up a lot of business.

When I sold prepaid phone cards, I would see a guy coming off a payphone at the airport and I would stop the person, and ask, "Excuse me, sir; I hope you don't mind my bothering you, but did you by any chance use a calling card when you used the phone?"

"Sure" or "Yes" they would say.

Then I would ask, "Which did you use? AT&T, MCI, or Sprint?"

They would tell me what they used, and I would respond by asking whether they would be interested in me helping them to save money on each call. Some were interested, and some asked me to get out of their faces. But the ones who wanted to explore my proposal stopped and talked to me. I took their info and followed up with them, and I became the biggest seller of these cards. It was an innovative approach to building business and it worked.

Selling from Within

After reading about all ten skills that you should practice, it should be clear that the overarching idea is that selling is a business. You are running your own business from within, so you need to develop yourself to be the best you can be. All these things we talked about take T.I.M.E. (Things I Must Earn).

It takes time, but once you have all this inside you, it's so much easier to sell. It makes your sales career so much more exciting that you want to continue. I never, ever want to stop selling. It's the best field I've ever chosen.

Equip yourself with knowledge. Equip yourself with what it takes to be a professional salesperson—not just someone who goes door-to-door and then falls apart. You don't fall apart in selling. There are good times, bad times, dry times, wet times—whatever it is, who cares? It's part of the selling, or being. Being in sales is not just a job. It's a business on its own. You have to understand the intricacies; every little part of this business.

Success comes from the moment you get your first "yes" and a person is buying from you. Success also comes when you've said "yes" to yourself, affirming that you can have the life you envision.

Say "yes" to yourself. When you say "yes" to yourself, then you can go out there and try it. Go make it work for yourself. When you get the first customer who says "yes," you'll continue on until the next customer says "yes" as well. Now, there are going to be a lot of "no's," but "no" only means "no" for now.

Most importantly, you're going to be successful if you're truly into helping other people get what they need and you believe you have the product or service they feel *they* need to be successful.

AUTHENTIC SELLING TIPS

1. Always be thinking about time management, database management, and prospecting. These are the most effective tools necessary for daily productivity and realizing long-term goals.

2. If you feel like your sales business is lacking, review the ten essential skills explained in Chapter Four: communication skills, customer service, interpersonal skills, empathy skills, goals, negotiation skills, decision making, creativity, referrals, and innovation.

FREEDOM QUESTIONS

1. What are the biggest time-wasters in your business? How can you eliminate them or make them productive?

_____

_____

_____

_____

2. What are the benefits of your product that specifically will help your customers solve their problems?

_____

_____

_____

_____

3. What is the biggest "No" you usually receive in your business or in life? How can you creatively think outside the box to turn that "No" into a "Yes"? Consider how better communication or negotiation skills might help in this process.

_____

_____

_____

_____

CHAPTER FIVE

REPRESENTING YOURSELF AS THE PRODUCT

"What you can do is ask:
'What is the value to the customer?
What are they willing to pay for?'
Then, deliver great products and services."

— Greg Brenneman

"I am the commodity and so are you."

— *David Stern*

I n this chapter, I want to bridge the ideas of self-development with sales fundamentals. So we're bringing together the first half of the book, which is more about the personal journey, with the distilled sales business basics of the previous chapter.

The topics reserved for this chapter aren't typically discussed in sales business education. In this section, I want to narrow our focus down to some unique and, often overlooked, bedrock ideas such as being overly comfortable in your business practices, building a clientele, and practical ways to streamline your day-to-day operation. I want to conclude Chapter Five by offering an enlightening sales perspective to employ when out in the field.

Lifting the Hood

Thirty years ago, I was at a crossroads. I was making a living, but I wasn't staking out a future for myself or my loved ones. Making a living means just paying the basics, like rent, utilities, and food. It's getting by, and since you're not feeling hunger pains, or in danger of being evicted, you can get used to this lifestyle and ignore some important deficiencies in the way you run your business.

For me, during this pivotal period, I realized I was getting too comfortable. It dawned on me that I had to commit and stay focused in order to change the way I thought about my goals. Otherwise, I was just like a horse with blinders on. I was following a narrow path without autonomy—someone else was cracking the whip while I was just aimlessly trotting forward. Sound familiar?

I always talk about the perils of comfort in my coaching intensives. Say your yearly earnings are $75,000 or more, and with this money, you have become comfortable, you are paying bills, maybe savings some, but then some life changes start coming on the horizon. Perhaps you're starting to think about retirement, college for your children, a wedding for your daughter or son, or maybe you're even dreaming of a vacation house. At this time, you are realizing that the money you are earning is no longer enough. The problem is that the amount of money you are earning has allowed you to become comfortable. Now you want to earn more, and if you are serious about what you want or need, you're going to have to get uncomfortable.

The first step toward change is metaphorically lifting up the hood and checking out your daily routine and business practices. Survey how the engine runs and how you move forward. One thing you will surely find is that, in order to earn more money, you're going to have to do more each day.

The place to start in your workday overhaul is time management and organization. You would be surprised how crafting a fixed daily schedule can alter your earnings. Divvy up the day, with definite time slots dedicated to database management, prospecting, product knowledge, networking, and paperwork/billing. Write this schedule down and stick to it. Also, and we will get into this later in the chapter, keeping a tidy work area is crucial to effective business.

If you analyze your work habits and the structure of your day, make the appropriate adjustments, and put in the hard work, you're going to see yourself hit the bull's eye. And when you get to your financial goal, you're going to be comfortable again. It's inevitable.

Don't Stop

I had a client the other day who told me about his company's summer barbecue contest. In order to earn an invitation to this prestigious and fun event, an employee had to sell sixteen life insurance policies. My client was overjoyed that he qualified to attend the barbecue.

I was curious about the mathematics of the event, so I inquired how much commission sixteen policies translated into. He divulged that he raised about $30,000 in commissions to earn his place at the delicious festivity.

I crunched the numbers in my head and said to him: "You earned $30,000 and gained sixteen brand new customers to get into a barbecue. Wow, that is so wonderful. Do you know how much barbecue you can eat for $30,000? Why did you stop?"

It may seem like a basic question, but it speaks to something within us all: we stop when we think we reach the finish line. Sure, it makes sense. The race is over. The goal is met. We were granted a meal at the company barbecue. But you shouldn't stop.

You should continue for the next six or seven weeks to build another sixteen cases, so you can have barbecue forever. It's not about the company; it's about you building a future beyond just making a living. It's about your goals, saving for that rainy day, or heaven forbid, that medical emergency that incurs out-of-pocket expenses.

The biggest problem salespeople have is that they stop selling after the big sweepstakes are over. It's as if you met your goal, ate your barbecue dinner, and now you're satisfied and content to go back to the income you had before. What many people don't realize is that if they were once capable of increasing their earnings, they shouldn't stop there.

Then there's the scenario where you set a goal to earn

$10,000 a month. The first ten days of the month, you earn the $10,000, so the next three weeks, you coast and don't push yourself to close any further deals. This is such myopic thinking. By pushing yourself further, you could make a surplus of sales and stow away a nice nest egg for your future. Alternatively, the extra earnings could help you through a dry month.

If you're working for the bigger picture, you don't stop selling after you earn $10,000. You stop after the month is over, and then you start your new month again, with another goal in mind.

Survival Mode Doesn't Work

I meet many salespeople who don't want to have a regular, non-sales job where they could earn $1,000 a week. They don't want to work nine to five at a company, or get up at 6:00 a.m. to get to the job on time. They want to have an easier life.

So they get into something in sales where they can earn $1,000 or more a week because it's easier to be in the selling business—selling jewelry, selling boxing equipment, selling trucking supplies, or selling life insurance. It's easier. All the person needs to do is sell a certain amount in order to make it. Selling is big business; more than a J-O-B, it's a lifestyle—a great career.

But that's just a person calling himself a salesperson

who is in survival mode. This thinking is flawed, and it will catch up to him. Why? Because as time goes on, expenses become higher, the cost of living is more expensive, the rent goes up, the groceries are going up, gasoline goes up, and, if you're still making the same $1,000 a week, there's a good chance you're not going to make ends meet.

The cost of living always goes up—be prepared; make more than you need so you can save and easily adjust to inflated prices.

Maintaining Your Customer Base

One simple way always to be building your business is through maintaining your customer base. If you buy a building that has fifty-unit apartments, and you don't hire a superintendent to make sure it's kept clean, neat, painted properly, and that the apartments are taken care of, the thing is going to fall apart before you know it, and you're going to lose the whole building. Likewise, if you have a database of customers that you're not maintaining and you're not taking care of them, you're going to lose those invaluable contacts.

When you just go from customer to customer, you're surviving. When you are developing and bringing in more products, you're bringing more services and maintaining your customer base. That's when you're thriving.

You're reaching higher goals. You don't go past that first step by just surviving. Surviving gets you through the day, and it goes month to month. You pay your expenses, and you made enough so you don't have to borrow on a credit card or take out a loan from the bank.

I want you to thrive. Right now, you may think you earn more than enough money—you can always pay your bills. Fine. You feel okay. But if you made more money, took the extra money, and put it into a fund to save for your child's college tuition, child's wedding, or an anniversary gift for the spouse, you would start feeling better.

Now that you're earning more, you're feeling better about yourself on the inside. You're not just surviving; you're thriving. You're getting better. You have goals. You're achieving goals, and when you achieve goals, your quality of life changes. You can go from an old jalopy to a new car. You feel good, you worked for it, and you appreciate what you've done. Your self-worth grows because you're doing things for yourself. It's not just in dollars and cents. It's about you.

Write down on paper what your goals and dreams are and commit them to memory. Focus on writing these down and repeat them daily so they're ingrained in your head. You must keep a handle on it.

A lot of resistance to breaking free of one's comfort zone goes back to what I mentioned in early chapters:

The Roller Coaster Effect. This is an idea that sales is an up and down wild ride. In good times, you're rocketing up, and in bad times, you're plummeting down. But the thing about a roller coaster is that it's just a ride; it's all fun. When you're scaling the mighty hill, enjoy it, but know you're going to be descending for a bit after that skyward jolt. Conversely, when you feel the bottom crumbling beneath you, as you go quickly downward, just know the pull down will thrust you back up.

I want to clarify that when sales are down, you need to take time to regroup mentally, analyze your career goals, tidy up your desk, write reports, go over your billing, send out emails, and strategize how to build your business. This way, you're making the most of an offseason, and you'll be ready to maximize opportunities when things start to heat up.

Living life on the roller coaster is a reality in sales. You can either enjoy it or dread it. Choose which one you want to do. In sales, we have choices. Why not enjoy the roller coaster?

A Wide Net

Building your clientele is a fundamental skill that's not touched upon deep enough in most sales seminars. Everyone faces this daunting task. Whether it's building a client base for a new venture or fortifying an established base, we all have to gather sympathetic contacts and turn those into prospects.

In the beginning, keep a sense of exactly who is the type of client who would benefit from your service or product. As much as I would encourage you to do this, I would also say cast a wide net. Trial and error can be a really effective tool, especially in the beginning.

Meeting new people and building fresh relationships is challenging. People will have all sorts of questions and concerns during those initial meetings, so you may feel overwhelmed. Don't. You're not expected to know everything; you're there to begin a relationship. All you need to do is be present in the conversation and sincere. If you get stuck, just respond by saying something similar to: "Bobby, that's a very good question. I don't have the answer for it. Do you mind if I get back to you within forty-eight hours with the answer?" And do get back to the person.

Honesty and truth resonate with people; they foster meaningful connections that can lead to long-term client relationships. A lot of salespeople go wrong here and feel like they have to supply an answer right then and there, so they lie or make up some phony answer. This response chips away at a good foundational client-to-salesperson interaction, and it may sully any future dealings or contact with the customer in question. Remember the old saying "Honesty is the best policy." It really is.

In a lot of industries, it takes four or five years to become a true sales professional. So don't put the pressure on yourself straight away to be a product expert, but do put the pressure on yourself to be an honest and forthcoming salesperson.

Striking Out

When you get down about beefing up your client database, think about the sport of baseball. Baseball players in the American League earn ten to thirty million dollars a year. How many times do these people strike out?

They don't hit the ball every time they step in front of the plate. Ball players strike out, many times—even the greats. Babe Ruth struck out more times than he hit homeruns. No one talks about his strikeouts; they only talk about the home runs. Sometimes, you'll hit a home run, a single, a double, or a triple. Sometimes, it might be best to bunt your way lightly to get onto first base.

We all strike out, so don't sweat it. When you're building relationships with people, it's almost like 90 percent of the time you get a "no," and 10 percent of the time you get a "yes."

They'll buy, or they won't buy, but you're building and

learning about the industry, and you're also learning transferable habits you can bring to any future endeavor.

The big trade secret in building a client base is making sure you have people's interests in mind. It's really that simple. Listen to what they need, and set aside thoughts of commission or company barbecues.

When you focus on other people's needs, you are building credibility, which is essential for turning a "no" into a "yes." Sometimes, this process takes time, but through it, you can accrue long-term clients who stay with you throughout your career. They'll trust you and always feel comfortable working with you.

One thing I always say to my clients is, "Know your clients." When you sell to people, always try to learn more about them. Do some initial preparation before that first meeting.

Today, we have the Internet, so you can Google any name, any company, and quickly obtain valuable information. If it's an individual, be sure to be respectful and don't dive into personal matters; in these instances, it's best to do a cursory Google search. Companies are obviously more public and have a lot of information online that you can use to get a clear a picture of your client.

Word-of-mouth business is a great way to build a network of customers. There is trust and comfort implicit in these connections since they're more intimate and personal. And because these referrals come from acquaintances, and even friends, it's easy to ask around and get information on them beforehand so you can better prepare for meeting them.

The Pathway to Closing

I can't stress enough the importance of listening to your customer's needs, acknowledging clearly that you understand them, and then offering solutions.

It's really that straightforward—that's the pathway to closing, but it takes time to develop this practice. So many times, we rush deals because we're desperate, lack confidence, or are arrogant and just assume we're going to close a deal. Always be a listener, a problem solver, and stay humble.

Once you establish rapport with a customer, you can have a monthly sale. But never take this for granted. Always be attentive, present, and sensitive to your client's changing needs. That's how you build a sales business. It's old fashioned, yes, but it works! And if you have a nice connection with a client, but you haven't closed a deal with him, fear not. Maintain the relationship, and when the client is ready for your product or service, he will come to you. Be patient.

Here's a story I want to share with you that feels appropriate and inspiring in this context. Years ago, when I was in jewelry, I tried to make inroads into the world of Macy's via its buying office in San Francisco.

To the company's credit, everyone was courteous and patient to me each time I presented my wares, but the appointments always ended with something like, "Oh, yeah, you've got some nice stuff, but we're currently okay."

It felt a little frustrating, but I'd say, "Do you mind if I call you again in six weeks if there's anything new?"

They'd tell me, "Not a problem."

I knew returning was what I needed to do to maintain and build the relationship, so I continuously went back with a reason to see them—a new product, a new type of color, a new this, a new that—whatever I could introduce to them. I kept building my relationship for three and a half years. It was always frustrating, but I kept showing up.

Finally, one day I got a phone call. Macy's was looking for a specific model, a specific type of chain. I said to myself, "Wait a second; three and a half years I've been chasing this client, and they never, ever gave me an order. Now they are looking for something, and they are calling me?"

So I asked them point blank, "You've known me for three and a half years; why all of a sudden did you decide to call me?"

The woman said to me, "At the time of your visits, we were contracted to seven vendors, and we couldn't do business outside those established relationships."

So as long as those vendors were keeping their promises, doing their thing, and giving the customer service they needed and staying innovative, Macy's was going to buy from them. Once one of the vendors failed in one of those areas, Macy's looked for another vendor.

The woman also told me, "Since you were so consistent for the last three and a half years, not forcing yourself on us to buy something but continuously showing us courtesy, we're ready to entertain your company as a vendor for us." My first order there was $46,000. That was a big victory for me.

When I analyze my demeanor in courting their business, I recall that I was never desperate to make a sale to Macy's, or to any prospect. It was just a prospect. My focus was on building relationships, and as I built relationships, I got hundreds and thousands of "no's." Always keep in mind that a "no" eventually leads to a "yes." If it's not today, it's tomorrow, it's the next year, or even three and a half years later, like with me and Macy's.

Investments and Dividends

Sometimes, it's best to think of relationships as investments that yield dividends with time. Take the immediate sale mentality out of your head. Think of building clientele as investing for the long term, the same way you buy a CD for five or ten years. Eventually, these investment options pay you a higher rate, but you have to do your time and let your money sit idle. You put money in a 401k for later, to pay off what's coming later. It's not for now.

I always encourage salespeople to be working with a broad array of clients. Have your larger customers and your small customers. The smaller accounts prepare you for the big ones. Also, sometimes a small victory might give you the strength and confidence to close a deal with a bigger customer.

Selling is a never-ending business. One of the things salespeople do is always look for new customers. We prospect. Sometimes, you can prospect a customer for years. I recently got a letter from a friend of mine in upstate New York who was chasing a client for seven years. She was constantly prospecting this client until she finally got a sale. I don't know many people who can say that. You know what? I don't know if I can say that. I recently got a client whom I saw four years ago, and every time I saw this person, it was because we ran into each other, or I called him every so often. Four years later, he decided to become a coaching client. Remember a "no" is a pathway to a "yes" if you just stay consistent, patient, and courteous. You'll get there.

Paperwork

Back in the '70s, when I was out there hustling in California and the Western states, we didn't have the luxury of computers and database management software like we have now. We worked off weekly or monthly planners. Inevitably, we would miss appointments or calls. It was a flawed system. Many promising leads got lost in a paper trail or were buried under piles on a messy desk.

During this time, I had an assigned territory that took me six weeks on the road to cover fully. When I came back from the circuit, I always managed to go to the beach or the pool, instead of doing paperwork, because it was easier and more fun.

What would end up happening was the piles grew bigger and bigger, and the bigger the piles got, the less I wanted to look at them. I found myself in this horrible pattern—I didn't want to organize the paperwork, but I needed to in order to get back on the road.

I soon realized that I wasn't capable of doing everything myself. There are certain things I'm good at, and there are certain things where I need help. So I hired a secretary who would come in for four or five hours a day to organize all my stuff. Then it would be a lot easier for me to do.

Today, I suggest to my clients that when all this minutia bogs them down, maybe it's time to hire someone to help with that type of work. That way, they can do what they're really good at, which is being in front of people, building relationships, talking to people, networking, and following up by making phone calls.

Let someone else do all the paperwork. It takes so much stress out of your life that it's unbelievable. I have a client who has three or four people in a support team. Each one does something different so together they're all cogs in the wheel that make this thing work really well.

A more cost-efficient way is a CRM (customer relationship management) program; you can use software like ACT or Salesforce for database management, time management, reminders to make your phone calls, etc. If you have a manageable business, are 1099 independent, or even if you're working for a company, if you have your own database management software, then you can sit in front of your computer and get organized.

You can control your time management, whom to call, when to call, and the reasons you call, and you can access notes that summarize the points of your previous call or meeting with the client. It's amazing what some of these programs can do and how much they can simplify your life and make you more productive.

Streamline Your Operation

When I first started in sales, I remember it was about

survival. There was a transition period between when I took notes and kept them on paper in books or planners and when the first computer came out.

I remember the first Commodore computer. I couldn't figure out how the hell to work it! I mean, it was so difficult for me because I wasn't used to it.

In these formative days of computer-based business, I held fast to my paper planner ways. I eventually bought a computer, and it was really difficult for me to learn. It wasn't as intuitive or user-friendly as today's machines are. If I had then what I have today, I think I could have maybe made ten times more money. Remember, in the 1970s, there were also no cellphones or beepers.

We didn't have all of that technology. It was a lot more difficult. Imagine if I had a computer and had been able to work then, the way we work today? With all these gadgets, you can get so much done without even leaving the office.

It was difficult transitioning to the computer era, but once I made the transition, it was a whole new ballgame. I remember the years when, if I wanted to look up prospects, I had to go through the Yellow Pages. When was the last time you saw a Yellow Pages? I don't even know if they print them anymore. Maybe they do. I don't know.

Today, you go online and you can Google anybody's

name and phone number. It's a lot easier to do the work today than it was thirty years ago. Take full advantage of technology and invest in it. If you feel out of step with it, maybe take some classes or hire an assistant or a secretary. The bottom line is, streamline your operation, in whatever way necessary, so you can do what you do best, which is building relationships and making sales.

You Are the Commodity

How do you see your career in sales? Is it a job? Or is it a career? Many powerhouse companies rely on salespeople. Heavyweights like IBM, Caterpillar, Deere, and Boeing couldn't exist without salespeople. Everybody uses salespeople.

If you have a sales career like I have, you can sell for any type of company. I can fluidly shift from selling jewelry for six years, to cellphones with Motorola, and I can shift again. How can I do this? Simple: My career is selling, and that's not tied to any product or service; it's tied to me and my strengths and weaknesses as a salesperson.

I don't have to rely on the company to feed me. I rely on myself to feed me. I'm an independent contractor. I can go to Motorola. Or I can go to World Telecom Group. Or I can work for myself. In each instance, you have to be really mindful of how to structure and operate your business.

For instance, in the business of telecom service, it's not a tangible product. I still represent the company that has a product and a service, and as long as its product and service is good, that's fine. But what happens if the company goes out of business? What happens if something happens? Does that mean that I'm done? I'm finished? No. That means I have to look for something else. Now, while I transition and look for something else, how do I live? Well, if you operate smart, you don't only work for bread and butter; you put money away for retirement and you put some money away for savings for nine to twelve months in case of emergency. Having a cushion helps you to look for the right opportunity between sales positions. You never want to be desperate.

I am the commodity and so are you. A lot of companies are looking for salespeople. Don't feel desperate to settle on one or feel like your life depends on the financial health of a company that employs you. We are professional career salespeople, and if we're good at what we do, a lot of varied opportunities are out there for us.

What we bring to the table is our expertise, our people skills, and our time-honored sales strategies. In some cases, we bring a whole database of clientele that can almost instantly reinvigorate a company's sales profile. I do my business, and the ways I conduct myself are my commodities. People don't buy the company name; they buy you. They want me, David Stern—not the name of the company I represent.

Does that mean that you can't be successful working for Big Pharma, or a company like Deere, Caterpillar, or Boeing? You definitely can. You can earn a base salary and commission, and together that could make for a great living. But you're also at the company's mercy.

Nobody Owns You

Sometimes, big companies cycle through salespeople. Consider the pharmaceutical industry. In that industry, if salespeople are earning too much money, the company may find someone to do the same job for less cost. That strategy might look good for the company's investors, but in the end, it hurts business because experienced salespeople are the lifeblood of incoming revenue.

I'll give you an example. My wife worked for a pharmaceutical company, earning $125,000 a year. The company decided to cut costs and laid off three thousand salespeople, including my wife. In her place, the company put in a less seasoned salesperson who earned $46,000 a year. The thing is that my wife has a life in sales and a robust contacts list. Those assets alone can actually help a company make a lot of money. Two months later, she found a new job. She was the commodity and didn't need that particular company to fund her life; she found another company to invest in her sales talents.

If you're building a career in selling, the relationships that you build will make you invaluable. You can go to work for any company, and you can represent any product or service, as long as you understand the products and the service well.

Now, if you worked for one company for ten years and just knocked on doors and made deals without distinguishing yourself, you're going to be in trouble should you experience a layoff.

What happens if you lose your job? Are you going to work in some storefront behind a counter for a meager paycheck? Are you going to get a J-O-B—just over broke—where you're paid just enough so you don't quit and you work just hard enough that you don't get fired. That's a different type of career. It's a different type of world.

When you're in sales, you're a business owner. You run your own business. My database is my database. Nobody else owns it—or me. That's what real selling is about.

A company can say, "David, I no longer want you to represent me. I don't want to pay you that kind of money." No problem! I'm not going to be happy about it, but no problem. I'll go find someone else who does appreciate what I can do for him, our relationship, and the way I conduct myself in the world of business because I'm a business owner.

Nobody can shut you down except yourself. Your boss can fire you. A company can say I no longer want to use your service. But do you ever hear of business owners firing themselves?

Presence

I want to conclude on a small point about you being the commodity: your presence. A first impression is everlasting. So mind your manners, stay off your cellphone during meetings, give a firm handshake, and look people in the eye when you speak to them. You can never go wrong this way. Also, look clean and well-groomed. Simple elegance also goes a long way in making a statement that you're a professional. It all goes back to that business axiom: Dress for the job you want, not the one you have.

A life in sales is empowering. Much of your success is really up to you, and no one or no company can take that away from you. Every day you better your life and your family's lives. You are the investment, so go out there and give it your all.

AUTHENTIC SELLING TIPS

1. Set realistic monthly goals for income and always push to go beyond those projected earnings. You never know when you will need a surplus of cash for something unexpected or for a joyous occasion.

2. No matter what, don't let yourself get too comfortable. Always be upping the ante, refining your financial goals, and striving to be more productive.

3. Remember in good times and bad times, what goes up, must come down, and what comes down, eventually goes back up. Stay focused on the big picture by creating a more lucrative and well-structured business; then you'll ride the roller coaster with ease.

4. If you lack organizational skills, investigate all the programs available to you now for billing, appointments, and database management. If you're not technology inclined, hire some help. Being organized is key to running a successful business.

5. In the business of sales, your career is based on your skills as a salesperson, not on the service or the wares you are selling. If you're an accomplished salesperson, you can literally sell anything.

6. If you're building a career in selling, and you're building relationships, that will make you invaluable. You can go to work for any company, and you can represent any product or service, as long as you understand the products and the service well.

FREEDOM QUESTIONS

1. On the lines below, create a daily schedule for yourself. Break it up into five categories: database management, prospecting, product knowledge, networking, and paperwork/billing. Break it into hour or half-hour time slots. (Don't forget lunch but keep it under an hour.) Follow this schedule for a week or two and then adjust it as needed. You may need certain things to be rearranged on Monday, compared to Tuesday, so that it evolves into a weekly schedule over time.

9:00 _____

9:30 _____

10:00 _____

10:30 _____

11:00 _____

11:30 _____

12:00 _____

12:30 _____

1:00 _____

1:30 _____

2:00 _____

2:30 _____

3:00 _____

3:30 _____

4:00 _____

4:30 _____

2. What is a realistic monthly goal for your sales income? When you consistently accomplish that goal, what will your next goal be?

_____

_____

_____

_____

_____

_____

_____

3. What other things can you do to be more organized and consequently, improve your sales abilities? List at least three here.

1. _____

_____

_____

2. _____

_____

_____

3. _____

_____

_____

CHAPTER SIX

KNOWING WHERE
YOU ARE GOING

"You simply have to put one foot in front of
the other and keep going. Put blinders on
and plow right ahead."

— George Lucas

"The day in the life of a salesman is about knowing where you're going and what you need to do."

— *David Stern*

What is a day in your sales life like? Are you rushing around breathless and disheveled, barely making scheduled appointments? Do you wake up with a grim outlook and start the day irritable? Did you get enough sleep the night before? In this chapter, I will discuss the ins and outs of a good day as a salesperson. This includes keeping to a fixed starting and ending schedule, how maintaining a positive outlook can increase your business, practical wisdom from my years on the road, and—the often neglected topic—keeping a healthy work-life balance.

What do you think is the difference between the deli on Main Street, the supermarket on Grand Street, and us as salespeople? The answer is: Nothing.

All businesses adhere to some fundamental principles. They all have a firm opening time and closing time that caters to the schedule of their clientele. If you own or run a grocery store, you might open up at six or seven o'clock in the morning when people need to buy a loaf of bread, cottage cheese, or a bottle of milk. You're going to close as late as possible because parents often send kids to the store to pick up missing items. You need to be open.

You also need to be ready for incoming business. You need to have inventory. Your store and its shelves have to be looking tidy and organized. Your help staff must well-groomed, alert, and ready to serve.

As salespeople, our store is us and our briefcase. We are like a migrating business; we have to go out to visit our clientele. We visit all the different supermarkets or stores, distributors or manufacturers, or whatever types of clients we might have.

Rainy Days

Run your sales business like anyone runs a business. You set a firm start time to accommodate your demographic. Before you officially open for business, make sure you're prepared for your customers. Know the clients you will be seeing, the most efficient way to travel, and be ready to pitch your wares.

A tip from the road is to know your planned route the night before. In my practice, I teach people how to set up their appointments according to the regions of the area or city where they're going to be. You have to be able to adjust your course depending on your particular location, and you will save yourself valuable time if you plan ahead. If it's the Tri-State area, plan a week or two in advance.

When you wake up in the morning, you know exactly where you have to be at 9:30 a.m. The day has a definite contour with firm appointments and meeting times. Your job now is just to be the best salesperson you can be. Everything happening that day is scheduled on the computer or in a notepad. You eat a good breakfast and get fired up for the day with some coffee. By the way, if you're a salesperson on the road, always have an extra shirt and tie in the car. I have one in the trunk that is wrapped in plastic just in case I pig out or I spill coffee on my nice white shirt.

The day in the life of a salesman is about knowing where you're going and what you need to do. Stay goal-oriented. Sitting and watching television, wasting time, reading blogs on the Internet, or reading the news is not goal-oriented.

Another thing to consider when facing the day is weather. It seems like a small thing, but bad weather can shape your attitude and your work ethic.

Some people see that it's raining and immediately assume it's going to be a nasty day. They have a negative attitude. Do stores close because of rain? Are employees at supermarkets snippy because of bad weather?

Every grocery, bakery, jewelry, and luggage store is open and functioning smoothly and pleasantly, rain or shine—it doesn't make a difference. Obviously, storms of epic proportions and very heavy snow affect all businesses. I'm not talking about these situations. I'm talking about regular rain, snow, and wintery conditions that make the salesperson's job more challenging.

Just because the weather is going to be nasty, should you allow it to ruin your day? Are you going to use bad weather as an excuse for not feeding your family? No. True salespeople are out there making a living. When I worked at Motorola, the New York City area used to have many of these large snowstorms. On those stormy days, I would purposely go out because I knew few salespeople took advantage of those days, and people were waiting for someone to knock on their doors.

If you're goal-oriented, no rain, sleet, snow, or storm is going to be in your way. Since we know some salespeople won't go out during bad weather, if you really want to get better, go out when nobody else does. People are going to love to talk to you. On sunny days, too many people come into the office, knocking on doors, but on days with nasty weather and less salespeople, the owners and managers will be more likely to want to hear what you have to say. Take advantage of that. Know where you're going and what you need to do.

Design Your Day

When you're going for lunch, go for lunch. We need to have a break. We've got to be easy on ourselves as well.

So, if you're going out for lunch, schmooze for half an hour or an hour. But anything over an hour with a friend for lunch and you will need to watch your calories. You're most probably going to eat more than you should, and now you're wasting time again because you're not supposed to be there. You're supposed to get on the road again to visit your clients. Long lunches equal wasting time, and they are not goal-oriented.

They used to say at Motorola, "If you come ten minutes early for an appointment, you're late." Showing up on time for an appointment or before the time for an appointment builds credibility. If you come in huffing and puffing because you were in traffic, that means you did not anticipate that issue in advance. When you come into your client's office, make sure your cell phone is turned off so you will not be disturbed. You will be able to pay attention to your client, and your client will notice that you are paying attention to him or her.

Design your day. I love to play a game of golf sometimes, so I put it in my schedule for any week or day when I have some extra time. I'll go out and play nine holes of golf with a friend of mine if I am meeting my goals and everything is running smoothly. Then I can afford to take the time off. It's important to be able to do something for yourself. You feel good about it, and when you feel good and you take care of yourself, you don't have to be stressed out twenty-four hours a day.

Have fun doing what you're doing, but stay organized.

When I come home at five or six o'clock at night, I talk to my wife. Then it's not about me; it's about her. I'll ask her, "How was *your* day?" I'll ask my kids, "How was your day?" After I'm done asking and knowing what their day was like, usually they ask me about my day. I might have had a crappy day. I might have had a great day. Either way, we can communicate. I might go on-line, but I already know my schedule for next week, so I'm cool, I'm chilled.

Remember, if you're in the business of selling, you need to have set hours. When are you going out there? Sometimes, we can start at six or seven o'clock in the morning. If I have to go to Upstate New York, it could take me an hour and a half to get to my destination. I've got to get up early in the morning, which means I've got to rest the night before, so I go to sleep early. Why? Because being rested helps me be focused. My brain has to be there. I shouldn't be tired. Schedule yourself accordingly.

Time Management: A Recipe for Success

Let's do a deeper dive into our "day in the life" analysis with a case from my own coaching practice. I had a client who was involved in four businesses but wasn't making any money.

The first thing we looked at was his time management.

He noticed he didn't get into his office until 11:00 a.m. There is a recipe for disaster! Then we took a look at the businesses, and we saw that two of his businesses were nonstarters. They weren't profitable and they didn't have much potential. This became a priority issue. Why continue focusing on these businesses? I asked him what would be possible if he would start his day earlier and shift his focus to the moneymaking ventures.

By following the suggestions I made, this client's life changed in the course of six or seven months. His whole life turned around because he obtained the knowledge of how to structure his day and what to focus on. He needed perspective; we all do.

Sometimes, you need an outside force to thrust you forward. You don't need to struggle, feel miserable, or stay in dead-end situations. Find a mentor, find a coach, or find someone who can help you get out of that misery. The client I just mentioned is very successful today. He's no longer thinking the grass is greener on the other side. He is now living a much better life.

I have many clients in different businesses—people whom I know have done well. Look at yourself; see what you're doing, and do some personal development. Look at yourself on the inside, look in the mirror, and get real. Stop making the excuses and watch what happens. Miracles happen.

You know, when I was out there, burning the rubber

off my shoes, and working all day chasing the business, burning the candle from both ends, I got into trouble. I couldn't focus or see where I was. I was lucky that, thirty years ago, I found myself a mentor who helped me to look in the mirror at what I was doing—where I was coming from, what skill sets I had, what skills I needed to develop—in order for me to go from step A to B to C to D to E.

Be Ready!

Don't think for one minute that it can happen for me or others, but that it can't happen for you. It *can* happen for you. You've got to be willing, and you've got to be ready. Unfortunately, many people will suffer for a very, very long time because they choose to be unwilling.

I believe in prayer, but I still have to do the footwork. I could pray from today until tomorrow, and it's possible that nothing will happen, but if I do the footwork, I stand a chance that things are going to happen—step by step, one by one, slowly but surely. If you look at other people, look at people who have suffered; all kinds of different things have happened to them, but they say, "I'm not going to let this bring me down because then I'm giving up on life." Why would you want to give up on life? Why would you want to give up on happiness? Why would you want to be a miserable SOB and come home and make your spouse and children miserable, too? That is giving up on life; why would you want to do it? Not only are you miserable, but everybody around you becomes miserable.

Positive thinking is an important component to a productive and fulfilling day. Your mindset in those first few hours of the day is really crucial to the outcome of your day. If you wake up angry, depressed, or with negative thoughts, that will pollute your day.

Start your day with calmness by getting up early and having everything organized for the day ahead. Not feeling anxious or late when going out the door will help you to feel upbeat and confident throughout the day.

I also want to say: Think about your thoughts. What do you think about? If you wake up feeling nervous about making ends meet or stressed that you're going to have a bad day, how healthy is that? If you are feeling less than or you are down on yourself, it only affects your performance.

Every day is another chance to close deals and improve your life. Every day is unique and can be what you want it to be. Be grateful to have this life; as a salesperson, you have freedom; you're in control. Salespeople don't have those glass-ceiling limits found in corporate or office life. You can make your dreams come true. Take your dreams, turn them into goals, design your roadmap, and stay optimistic and upbeat. That's how you climb the ladder of success.

Stay Energized

Have you ever bought rechargeable batteries? You may think: "Well, these will outlast regular batteries. I won't have to buy batteries ever again." But even rechargeable batteries run out of juice. Everyone eventually needs a break, especially salespeople.

We're human beings. We work hard, and we run out of juice sometimes too fast. We have to recharge. The way we do that is by taking care of ourselves daily. If we have a normal breakfast, lunch, and dinner, and we sleep for six, seven, or eight hours a night, or however much time we need, we won't run out of energy so fast. A vacation every once in awhile is always good. Recharging ourselves is how we live. It is how we exist.

In sales, the intensity is high because you're putting out a lot more energy. You're burning up a lot more energy than people who are standing on their feet or sitting behind a counter on a daily basis from nine to five. Your brain is moving faster and your emotions are driven all day long. You tire quickly, so you need to be careful and make sure you're taking care of yourself. Working all day long, and for some, partying all night long, means that, sooner or later, you're going to burn out. And it happened to me. I've experienced times when I was working and making money from a lot of sales. I'd go out to the clubs at night, have a good time, and not even think: *I need energy for the next day!*

Well, guess what? This choice ends in a hangover. How are you going to get up the next day and have the same energy? How long can you continue living like that without getting into trouble? It's going to come back to bite you in your rear end one day. It did for me. I had to stop, but I only stopped after I stopped doing so well.

I had to look at myself in the mirror and ask, "What's going on here?" I realized my time management was a little off. Yeah, I can go out every once in awhile, but to go out after a great day and party until late at night doesn't work well. I burnt a tremendous amount of energy and had a couple of beers thinking that they would replenish that energy.

Now what? I slept off the few beers, and the next morning, I had a hard time getting up. I didn't see at the time how it was going to kill my days, my weeks, and my months. So the only time I really saw it was when sales started to slip. Income started to slip. I only saw it when it was a little too late, so I had to make a change. I was burning the candle at both ends. It doesn't work.

I learned it's important to leave the work situation at five or six o'clock without going to the other extreme of going out all night. Spend time with your family. Or if you're single, go and relax, or watch some television. It's so important to take care of you and to recharge that battery in a healthy way. Go to the gym. When I go, I release a lot of tension because being in sales is not easy. Many times, you're getting "no's" all day long. You get rejected. You get stressed. When I am on the treadmill for forty-five minutes, a lot of that stress is released. I feel good. I come home, I take a shower, and I go to sleep. I rest. The next morning, it's a brand new challenge. It's a new roller coaster ride. The roller coaster operates from the morning until the evening. Every day, it's a new ride.

Kick the Tires

One of the fortunate things I have today is a lot of energy. I love to be out there talking to people. I love to contribute to the goals I have. I love the work I do, but every couple of weeks, I need to kick back and check in with myself. I've been doing this for the last five or six years, especially with my coach. I sit back and ask myself, "What's working? What's not working? What works well? What works not so well? Do I need to eliminate anything? Do I need to change anything? What do I need to do to make it work better, or does it pay? If it's not worth it--let's drop this, but let's not waste energy on stuff that's not working so well." You can't be analyzing everything on a daily basis, but I set up a time for it with my coach every two or three months. Talking with him helps me put everything in perspective and realign my efforts with my goals. Then

I feel less stressed, more focused, and able to chill out.

For the first five years when I was out in California, representing the jewelry firm, I'd come back from the road and process what I had accomplished. I'd ask myself, "What and where can I do better?" Then I would recharge my battery, swim a little bit, exercise a little bit, eat right, relax more, but I also focused on my business to see what was working and what was not. That way, I could go out on the road again with more energy to burn the rubber off my soles. Every six to eight weeks, I would make sure to check in with myself to make sure all the parts were working.

When I worked at the World Telecom Group, I would tour the country and give sales seminars. I went out to train salespeople on specific ways to sell their products. Every night, from Monday through Thursday, I was in another city.

In the morning, I'd get up, pack my bags, fly to a different city, talk to managers of the territory, and then give a big seminar. I would go to sleep at midnight or 1 a.m. and get up the next morning. I was on the run. I would do this for five or six weeks straight. I'd come back home and see what had developed in those weeks in the territories I was in. I'd rejuvenate and tweak my training methods. I'd ask myself, "What could I, should I, or will I change in my next training? I tried to find out what worked and what didn't work from different parts of the country, and then I would see whether I could adapt it.

Evaluate and assess your business. Every business, at the end of the month, needs to know whether it is profitable. With most big businesses, if you watch the business networks, there are earning seasons. How much in earnings did a business have last quarter or year? When you're involved in sales and you are your own business, you need to do this more often than just once a year. So look at your business, check in with your goals, and see whether it's working okay, whether you are up or down any percentage points compared to last year.

If you're doing your job right, and if you're working your territory really well, you can afford to take that little bit of time off to double-check that everything is running smoothly. It's like being a truck driver— if you've ever driven across the country, you will see these guys kick their tires. They have this stick that they hit the tires with to make sure the tires have enough air. We need to check out the tires. We need to check our business to make sure we're fully functional; that there's nothing that's fallen behind. We need to check on our follow-up schedule, time management, and product knowledge on the different mechanisms turning the wheels of our business.

And sometimes, we need to take a vacation for a week or two to go away with the spouse or family because that's a part of living. That's what we work for, and what we do. We need to go away with our significant other to take a break and relax.

Work Smarter, Not Harder

At a Fortune 100 company I represented, we had a quota system. Our sales were based on weekly, monthly, and quarterly goals. We needed to create "X" amount of sales for each period. As salespeople, we run on energy. If we don't have the engine working 100 percent, we can't perform properly. My manager always kept track and always asked, "How many prospects did you see? How many customers did you add to your base?" Many times, I was out of energy, and when that happened, it was obvious that I was doing it the wrong way because perhaps I wasn't focused. It led my manager to ask me, "Are you really doing what you say you are doing?"

When we're young, we don't pay attention to what twenty years down the road is going to look like. We have no clue. Some of us are lucky that every five years we can look back to see how things went so we can make the next five years better—perhaps more lucrative. Yet, we constantly need to be changing. We're aging. We're getting smarter.

It's not that we need to work harder, just smarter. So when you're out there, and you're twenty years old, just getting into the field and the business of selling or anything else that you want to do, it's going to be different than five or ten years from now.

Remember to focus and keep working on yourself. It's like when you build a puzzle. If you have a puzzle that has 1,250 pieces, you're not going to finish it right away. You're not going to build it in one day. It's going to take time, and as the time goes on, you can see more of the image. You can see, let's say, a house in the country with a white picket fence, two cars, a lawn, trees, birds, and a little pond with some goldfish. Whatever that big puzzle is—the more time you put into it, the more you put the pieces together—the more you see the picture of what you worked for all these years.

Remember, you are the commodity. In this instance, I want you to invest in yourself by treating yourself well. Eat healthily, sleep enough, purge out negative thoughts, plan ahead so you don't have to rush, and, last but not least, take time out to recharge and fill up your soul. The work-life balance isn't just crucial to being productive; it's essential to being a good spouse, parent, friend, and a self-aware person. Now, go out there and make your dreams happen!

AUTHENTIC SELLING TIPS

1. Plan each day thoroughly, which means having a firm schedule of appointments, an efficient travel route, and breaks in the day to eat and catch your breath.

2. Take advantage of nasty weather conditions because the competition often stays home, giving you opportunities to get an edge with prospects, and drum up more business.

3. Be prepared for anything. This means always bring an extra shirt and tie, and always show up early for appointments.

4. Take care of yourself in every way. Moderation is key with a work-life balance. Negative thinking, rushing around, and disorganization can pollute your mindset during the day. Wake up calm and collected, and try to reflect on your experiences. Positive thinking promotes productivity.

FREEDOM QUESTIONS

1. What types of unexpected events might happen in your day, such as bad weather or spilling food on your shirt? What can you do to plan ahead for these situations?

_____

_____

_____

_____

_____

_____

_____

2. What negative things do you tell yourself each day? Write them below. Then write a positive sentence you can replace it with.

Negative example: I'm always stressed. I just don't have enough time to do everything. Positive example: I'm grateful that I have so much work and my income reflects that abundance.

Negative: _____

Positive: _____

Negative: _____

Positive: _____

Negative: _____

Positive: _____

3. It's important to spend time reviewing and evaluating your business and how you're doing. To get you started, I've included the Essential Skills Sets for Leaders and Entrepreneurs checklist in the Bonus Section at the end of this book. On the line below, write down the time you will commit to performing this evaluation. For example, every third Thursday of the month at 8 a.m.

_____

4. What is one thing you can start doing on a regular basis for yourself to rejuvenate and make sure you don't run out of energy?

_____

_____

_____

_____

_____

_____

_____

_____

_____

_____

_____

_____

_____

_____

CHAPTER SEVEN

FIGHTING FOR YOUR FREEDOM

"IT ISN'T UNTIL YOU BEGIN TO FIGHT IN YOUR OWN
CAUSE THAT YOU BECOME REALLY COMMITTED TO
WINNING AND BECOME A GENUINE ALLY OF OTHER
PEOPLE STRUGGLING FOR THEIR FREEDOM."

— ROBIN MORGAN

*"There's a thing called life, and as long as I'm alive,
I have to do everything in the world to make my
life the best it can be."*

*— Herman Stern, Auschwitz survivor
and the author's father*

You will have noticed, over the course of this book, that I have talked a lot about the importance of freedom. A lot of times, freedom is within our reach, and we don't even know it. It's facing us, staring us in the face, and we are blind to it. Sometimes, we are the ones who deprive ourselves of freedom. Sometimes, we don't even know that we're not happy: We just exist.

We lock ourselves in a prison with our thinking, with our behavior, with our fears, and with our lack of ambition. We want out of this predicament, we want to live better or happier, but we don't know how to go about it. So we create this prison for ourselves. I've been in that prison quite a number of times over my life. For a few years, I found myself in a prison of my own making.

I talk about the prison when I see my clients are hanging out in one; I can see it because I've been there. That's when I ask, *"Are you for real?!"*

Surviving Against All Odds

When I was a kid growing up in Brooklyn, I heard the stories of the people who lived through World War II, specifically from my father. He would tell stories of where he came from, what happened to him, his mom, his dad, and his siblings. We sat around the table on many a Friday night, having dinner. I remember when I was with my father, being curious about his father, his mother, and his family; I wanted to know about where he came from, where he grew up, and I was always asking questions about it, so he'd talk about his father. He'd talk about his mom, and he'd talk about his nine sisters. I remember vividly, as a little kid, saying, "Where are they? Where are they now? How do I get to them? When can I meet them?"

But he told me that I couldn't because of what had happened. And then he talked about World War II. He started to talk about how people were taken away from their homes, and they were put on these cattle cars. As a little kid, I didn't understand what he was talking about. All I knew was that he had sisters, so I said, "When can I meet my aunts? When can I meet my cousins?" Later on, as I grew older, and I heard more about those stories, I got to be more interested in them because I wanted to know more details of what had happened. What had happened to these people?

My father told me how he had been a prisoner of war,

about being in Auschwitz. That's what he talked about when, every few years, we'd have a discussion about it. And it was horrifying because, as a young child, I couldn't comprehend what I heard. I couldn't emotionally feel what he was saying. It wasn't until I got older and I started to hear him talk about losing nine sisters, a mother, and a father in a concentration camp—they were burnt in a crematorium—that I realized what he told me. I started to think: Oh, wow. How did you get lucky? How did you stay alive?

I remember him telling me many stories about the war. One was about how when he was sixteen, he got to Auschwitz. He was in line with his mother and sisters, while the Nazis were choosing who would go to the left or to the right. His mother told him, "Go, go, and go! Run! Go to the other side." He let go of his mother's hand, and he ran to the right. After he got to the other side, he came face to face with the notorious Mengele, who asked him, "How old are you?" My father told him he was eighteen. He was really sixteen, but eighteen came out of his mouth. So they sent him to the right, which meant he went to a labor camp, rather than the crematorium.

A few years ago, my father asked me to join him on a business trip to Germany. I turned around and said, "I'd love to join you, but on one condition: once we're done with work, we're going to take some time off because I want to go see the sites that you always told me about." He had always talked to me before about the camp and after the war. He had talked to me about how he dug the big pit for the war camp he was in. I asked him to show me the concentration camp. I said, "They have all these museums; let's go see this."

I was somberly excited when he agreed. I took my camera, and I was prepared, because the work was just work, but I was going to learn about a piece of my father, a big part of his past that I had heard so much about. I thought about how, fifty years later, I was finally going to be able to put my eyes on something, actually visualize what he was talking about instead of imagining it, and to me, that was tremendous. It was scary, but I was excited to go.

Leaving Hanover, Germany, after we did our business, we flew to Munich, rented a car, and drove to a town called Kaufering. Kaufering was the last work camp my father lived at before Dachau. I couldn't wait to get there. In Germany on the Autobahn, there's no speed limit; I was in the left lane, speeding the hell out of that car. I had rented a nice vehicle, and I drove at top speed because I could and it was legal. Besides, I was going to get there faster. We wound through the roads, and my father knew exactly where we were going. When we got to this small town, we parked the car because we couldn't go up the hill any further, so we walked up the rest. And at the top, I saw this humongous, open pit, stretching as far as one can see, like the size you would dig for a big project, such as the Empire State Building or a Twin Tower, something like that, except ten times the size. All there was to see was this big, deep, hollow pit.

My father said, "David, this is where many others and I were working. We labored hard, shoveled, and dug here for no reason, and we still don't know why. Nothing ever happened with it. This was a labor camp. For all the other prisoners and I, who were here digging, and digging, for no obvious reason, all we saw was nothing, just a big empty space."

Then he said, "Come across the street. We need to go into the woods. I'm going to show you where I helped bury friends, people who were working in the labor camp who unfortunately died."

I walked with him for about half an hour, into the woods, through the snow. It was mid-January, so the snow was not knee deep; it was waist deep, sometimes even higher than waist deep, in some places chest deep, but we walked through it just to get into the wilderness. Then, all of a sudden, I saw the spot where the big tombs were located, where hundreds and thousands of people were buried. Some of my father's good friends were buried there.

From there, we went to the outskirts of the city named Dachau. Dachau was one of the worst camps the Germans built. I was there during one of the coldest months of the year, and chills went down my spine.

I had come to this vast, gated area surrounded with electric barbed wire that housed the Holocaust museum. Just seeing this, before even entering, was the worst thing in the world to see. In the great space, you see the outlines of the bunkers. There's one original bunker that's open for visitors, and you can see where every bunker was standing and the big sign that says, "Arbeit Macht Frei," meaning "Work gives you freedom."

My father led me to the bunker. I was so scared to be in this thing. This was where people slept. Instead of bunk beds, they had triple bunk beds, skimpy little things. And the old wood that they had was still there. I said, "This is where you lived?"

"Yes, in one of these, on top over there."

I could only ask, "What was going on?"

"People were dying in their beds. People were suffering, dying, and it was horrifying. It was horrifying to see this."

I was stone cold; I couldn't believe this had happened. This was the place my father spent time in? I held onto his hand like I was a five-year-old kid, and he told me these stories again, and then at the end, he said to me, "You know, why don't you wait outside? I want to pray my afternoon prayers."

My father is a very religious man. He prays in the morning, in the late afternoon, and in the evenings. I said, "Dad, why do you want to do it inside? Why don't you do it outside?"

He told me, "Just let me be."

And I stepped out. When I looked in from the window, my father was completely involved in his prayers. I looked at his face from the side, through the window, and I couldn't believe what I was seeing. What was going on here that was taking so long? You could see on his face that his mind was somewhere else—maybe fifty years prior, maybe reliving it all as he stood there. Every second was minutes, and minutes were hours. It was so painful to see him at this moment, and I was scared because I was looking at my watch every few minutes, and I knew this place was closing at 5:00 p.m., that we had a long way to walk to get out of the gates and back to my car.

Finally, *finally,* he came out, and I looked at his face, and I said, "Dad, we've got to get out of here because they're going to lock us in here; it's almost 5:00 p.m. We only have a few minutes."

My father turned around, looked me in the face, and said, "David, they didn't keep me in then. They're not going to keep me in now."

That was such a powerful statement. Don't worry about it. We'll be fine. We'll be okay. We will get out on time. And we just walked out of there. For me it was like,

"Let's get out of here. Let's get out of here. This is such a cold, eerie place. Let's get out of here." And I kept thinking about how he was in there for all that time.

When my father was a prisoner in this camp, how many times did he think, "Let's get out of here. How do we get out of here? When, and will we ever, get out of here?" When the prisoners saw all the concrete walls, barbed wire, and the double-barbed wire fences, they must have thought there was no way in the world to get out. Yet we walked right out of the prison at Dachau.

Afterwards, we went from Dachau to Feldafing, which was a DP camp for prisoners who survived the war, and we tried to get in. It was changed to a military base after the war, and I met an old man who helped me get in to see a building that my father recognized because it was the only original building that still existed over there. At the end, my father said, "This is what it was like, but I was able to get out, and I don't have to be there anymore."

From then on, I was able to connect and stay connected to my father by being able to look at what he went through on his own. He lost his mother, his father, and his nine sisters. They were all burnt in the crematoriums. My father survived as a young boy, eighteen years old by the time the war was over, and then he had to create his own life.

Why in the world would he want to do anything after

that? In my mind, he had all the reasons in the world to be drinking alcohol all day long. He could have thought: What was the point? But he always knew that there was more to life. He has always told my family, "There's a thing called life, and as long as I'm alive, I have to do everything in the world to make my life the best it can be."

He committed to starting his life all over again. He told himself, "If I want to participate in life, to start all over again, to have children, I have to get married and I have to work hard and be supportive. I have to go through life on life's terms. I have to stay committed." Today, my father is eighty-seven years old, and if you want to meet with him at ten in the morning, he's in his office.

When my father was in the DP camp, with other survivors from the labor camp, they all stuck together. Later, he went to France to study and to be in a place where young homeless boys without parents were after the war. There the boys were helped to come to America. One of my father's best friends, a rabbi, moved to Brooklyn and told him he was going to help bring him there. My father had nothing. He had no clothes, no money, no parents, no brothers, and no sisters. He had nothing in the world. He spoke Yiddish and Hungarian.

My father had an uncle in America who found out he was alive and sent him five dollars. Out of the five dollars, my father spent $4.90 on used clothes and shoes, something so he could look normal. He boarded the ship in France with ten cents to his name. Ten cents—can you imagine? And he knew that when he arrived in America, he'd take a train to the address he had on a piece of paper, and at that time, the train cost five cents.

At the time, my father was about twenty years old. And guess what? With his whole fortune of ten cents being on this boat for weeks going to America, guess how he spent half his fortune? He saw that other passengers were drinking Coca-Cola, so he got curious. What was so good about Coke? People were drinking it. So he wanted to have one. They told him it cost a nickel. He spent half his fortune on a Coca-Cola, so the only nickel he had left was for buying a token to ride the train. He had absolutely nothing. He didn't have a suitcase, just a bag with some clothes in it. But he came to New York, to the free country, for the opportunities and freedom he had heard about in stories.

When he visited his older uncle, he had a place where he could stay. He went back to school again, and after a while, he knew he wanted to get married, build a family, and start his life all over again. That's what everybody was doing, and that's what he decided he was going to do. He told himself, "I'm going to do it despite whatever happened to me. I'm going to build a family. I'm going to make a life for my family. That's what I'm going to do, what I'm committed to do." He was goal-oriented. He was introduced to my mother, and they got married. They had a dinky little apartment, which my father worked three jobs in one day to pay the rent on, and then he started having children.

One day, he got into business with my mother. My mother was the person who spoke better English. My father picked up words here and there, so she taught him to speak English. I think he went to school a little bit, part-time, to learn some English, too. My mother was the salesperson in the company. My father was the administrative part of the company, and they individually worked hard all day, and sometimes even late at night, to try to achieve their dreams. As the kids started to grow, my father began to see the joy of what he had created for himself in his family. My older brother is named after my father's father, and my only sister is named after his mother. To him, it was the biggest thing in the world to have children and name them after his father and mother. What an accomplishment!

Your Prison

Let me ask you a question. You might not be in that prison, and you might not be in such a painful prison as my father was in, but have you created your own prison? I did. It's my own Auschwitz, my own Dachau. We all create our own prisons. We don't think along those lines, but in actuality, when we're not happy and we're miserable, we're in prison.

Look at the difference. For my father, it was a prison that had double-wired fences that one could never, ever dream of escaping, and many, many people around him were dying. It was just a matter of time whether he was going to die or not. Luckily, the American government freed Dachau, so he was able to get out. He was still homeless, and he was still poor, but he had a breath of fresh air because he was somewhat outside the prison. In a way, though, he was still a prisoner because of the questions: Where do I go, and where do I get food? When he was in one of the concentration camps, he found rotten apple and potato peels in the garbage, and that's what people fought over to eat.

Slowly, but surely, he picked up the pieces of his life. He struggled, but he became totally free. During this time, he had his ups and downs: He didn't know whether he was going to eat breakfast, lunch, and dinner. Who knew where the food was going to come from? Slowly, but surely, he put the pieces together because he knew he wanted to be free, to survive, and to live. My question to you is: How much do you want to live?

We all want to live. We have food. We have everything, but if you actually want to reach your goals, you need to get out of the prison. We lock ourselves in the prison, we make excuses for ourselves, and those excuses don't allow us to function properly. So what's the difference between being in Dachau or being here? The difference is that the door in our prison doesn't have a lock. There is no fence, and there's no barbed wire. You *can* get out.

If you're in sales, you ride the roller coaster. You go up and you go down. So what? This is part of what we do, what we live for, but look at the freedom we get from being in sales. Look at the freedom we get from achieving the goals we set. I realized thirty years ago that it was me who put myself into prison. I choose not to be there, and I am no longer a prisoner. We have people helping us get out. We have mentors, coaches, and sales managers. If we don't realize that we're in our self-created prison, we're not going to get out. We have to do that from within.

Some of the most beautiful things I have in my life are my discussions with my father. We travel sometimes, and I talk to him. I ask him, "What helps you keep going? What helps you on a daily basis?" He says, "I know where I came from, and I'm reminded constantly where I came from, and I know that I don't want to be there. I don't want to go back to where I was. I constantly need to keep on walking to improve and better my life, to keep on going forward."

We don't have to look at and live in all the negative stuff that happened to us. We don't have to keep it in the back of our minds. We don't want that, in fact. I need to go out and do what I need to do on a daily basis to achieve the goals I want. We can all do it.

There's a saying: Misery is optional. You don't have to be miserable. You can be happy and do what you need to do. Just keep making progress and moving forward. When you move forward, you achieve one goal and then another and another goal, and you just keep on building. You're building yourself, your family, your friendships, and your relationships with people. Many people are living happy lives, so why not you?

Why not?

ESSENTIAL SKILL SETS FOR LEADERS AND ENTREPRENEURS

Your success in any job depends on the value of your contribution to the organization. Managers, mentors, and professional coaches can encourage, advise, and guide you as you grow professionally. However, the ultimate responsibility for your career development is yours and yours alone.

The statements listed below describe the consistent actions of individuals who are well-developed in the competencies needed to be successful in sales and life. They are adapted with permission from Mr. Bill Bonnstetter of Target Training International.

I suggest you use these statements as a guideline for

checking in with yourself on a regular basis, perhaps monthly, to see what your strengths are and which items you need to work on. After completing the self-assessment, pick the three or four items that you most need to work on and make them your focus for the next month. In thirty days, return to the list to see where you have made progress and what you still need to work on. (To make this easier for you, I have copies of this list at my website www.CoachStern.com that you can print out each month to use.) Do not hesitate to contact me, hire a coach, or find a mentor to help you if you feel stuck.

As you look through the list, rate yourself on a scale of 1-4 as follows:

☐ 4 = Excellent
☐ 3 = Good, but can be better
☐ 2 = Needs serious work
☐ 1 = Must begin doing immediately

Goal Orientation: Energetically focusing efforts on meeting a goal, mission, or objective.

_____ Acts independently to achieve objectives without supervision.

_____ Expends the necessary time and effort to achieve goals.

_____ Recognizes and acts on opportunities to advance progress toward meeting goals.

___ Establishes and works toward ambitious and challenging goals.

___ Develops and implements strategies to meet objectives.

___ Measures effectiveness and performance to ensure results are attained.

___ Acts with a sense of urgency to achieve goals.

___ Demonstrates persistence in overcoming obstacles to meet objectives.

___ Takes calculated risks to achieve results.

Persuasion: Convincing others to change the way they think, believe, or behave.

___ Utilizes the knowledge of others' needs, wants, beliefs, attitudes, and behavior to promote a concept, product, or service.

___ Builds trust and credibility before attempting to promote concepts, products, or services.

___Understands and utilizes compliance-producing behaviors that influence others such as authority, being likeable, proof of the prior compliance of others, limited availability, and sampling or giving something away to create a sense of obligation.

___ Uses logic and reason to develop rational arguments that challenge current assumptions, attitudes, beliefs, and behaviors.

___ Identifies and addresses the social, emotional, economic, and practical barriers that prevent people from complying.

___ Adapts techniques and approaches to the needs and wants of those being influenced.

Personal Effectiveness: Demonstrating initiative, self-confidence, resiliency, and a willingness to take responsibility for personal actions.

___ Possesses unwavering confidence and belief in personal capabilities.

___ Takes initiative and does whatever it takes to achieve goals.

___ Projects confidence and self-assurance.

___ Bounces back after setbacks.

___ Asserts self in personal and professional life.

___ Admits mistakes and works to avoid repeating them.

___ Accepts personal responsibility for achieving personal and professional goals.

___ Functions effectively and achieves results even in adverse circumstances.

Planning/Organizing: Utilizing logical, systematic, and orderly procedures to meet objectives.

___ Works effectively within established time frames and priorities.

___ Utilizes logical, practical, and efficient approaches.

___ Prioritizes tasks for optimum productivity.

___ Develops procedures, processes, and systems for order, accuracy, efficiency, and productivity.

___ Anticipates probable effects, outcomes, and risks.

___ Develops contingency plans to minimize waste, error, and risk.

___ Allocates, adjusts, and manages resources according to priorities.

___ Monitors implementation of plans and makes adjustments as needed.

Interpersonal Skills: Effectively communicating, building rapport, and relating well to all kinds of people.

___ Strives for self-awareness.

___ Demonstrates sincere interest in others.

___ Treats all people with respect, courtesy, and consideration.

___ Respects differences in others' attitudes and perspectives.

___ Listens, observes, and strives to gain understanding of others.

___ Communicates effectively.

___ Sensitive to diversity issues.

___ Develops and maintains relationships with many different kinds of people, regardless of cultural differences.

Customer Service: Anticipating, meeting, and/or exceeding customer needs, wants, and expectations.

___ Strives to anticipate, identify, and understand customers' wants, needs, and concerns.

___ Responds to customers with a sense of urgency.

___ Follows through on customer requests.

___ Is patient and courteous with customers.

___ Resolves issues and complaints to customers' satisfaction.

___ Expends extraordinary effort to satisfy customers.

___ Develops relationships with customers.

___ Partners with customers to assist them in achieving their objectives.

___ Acts as an advocate for customers' needs.

___ Takes professional risks for the sake of customers' needs.

Self-Management (Time and Priorities): Demonstrating self-control and an ability to manage time and priorities.

___ Effectively manages emotions and impulses.
___ Effectively manages time and priorities to meet deadlines.
___ Presents self assertively.
___ Demonstrates an ability to maintain composure in the midst of crisis.
___ Strives for continuous improvement.
___ Balances personal and professional life.
___ Takes initiative and acts without waiting for direction.
___ Accepts responsibility for actions and results.

Flexibility: Agility in adapting to change.

___ Responds promptly to shifts in direction, priorities, and schedules.

___ Demonstrates agility in accepting new ideas, approaches, and/or methods.

___ Effective in juggling multiple priorities and tasks.

___ Modifies methods or strategies to fit changing circumstances.

___ Adapts personal style to work with different people.

___ Maintains productivity during transitions, even in the midst of chaos.

___ Embraces and/or champions change.

225

Continuous Learning: Taking initiative in learning and implementing new concepts, technologies, and/or methods.

___ Demonstrates curiosity and enthusiasm for learning.

___ Takes initiative in acquiring and mastering the skills and knowledge requirements of a position.

___ Keeps abreast of current or new information through reading and other learning methods.

___ Actively interested in new technologies, processes, and methods.

___ Welcomes or seeks assignments requiring new skills and knowledge.

___ Expends considerable effort and/or expense on learning.

___ Genuinely enjoys learning.

___ Identifies applications for knowledge.

___ Is considered a knowledgeable resource by others.

Empathy: Identifying with and caring about others.

___ Demonstrates genuine concern for others.

___ Respects and values people.

___ Perceives and is sensitive to the emotions people experience.

___ Expends considerable effort to understand the real needs, concerns, and feelings of others.

___ Advocates for the interests, needs, and wants of others.

___ Demonstrates cross-cultural sensitivity and understanding.

___ Takes personal and/or professional risks for the sake of others.

ABOUT THE AUTHOR

DAVID STERN is an esteemed sales coach who brings over forty years of sales experience to each of his coaching sessions. His methodology combines from-the-field wisdom, insights on interpersonal dynamics, perspectives on self-development, and systematic evaluation methods to forever change other people's selling careers. He works one-on-one using custom client programs that yield real results.

In addition to these pragmatic tools, a foundation of Stern's work is belief––belief in the value of the work and the value of the self. "When you meet sales superstars, they exude this quiet confidence," says Stern. "Lack of confidence holds people back."

Looking back on his sales career and the lessons he has valued the most, Stern says: "Success in this business comes down to awareness, self-acceptance, self-development, communication, belief in yourself and the service you provide, and most importantly, it comes down to being honest and caring."

Find out more about David Stern at:

www.CoachStern.com

ABOUT
DAVID STERN'S
COACHING

David Stern has one of the most effective approaches to increase sales numbers in career coaching because of the expansiveness and thoroughness of his work.

Each client's coaching journey begins with an assessment evaluation test. Through studying these results, David tailors a rigorous plan comprehensively culled from the breadth of the business. This curriculum balances essentials and basics with enlightening self-development tenets designed to stretch you and make you reach out of your comfort zone to attain higher numbers than imagined.

David's one-on-one work is rigorous and geared toward getting his clients back out into the world armed with the tools to succeed.

Coaching Methodology

Breaking Out

When you get comfortable in your career, your numbers begin to taper off. The problem is, your standard of living has now gone up—and you want more, but you don't have the drive to knock on doors to get more. The best way to combat this cycle is to break out of your comfort zone, and push yourself to raise your numbers. David Stern helps to get you through career stasis via his solid program of sales basics and enlightening perspectives on the art of sales.

Are You For Real ?!

One of the most powerful tools we have in business is self-reflection—simply looking in the mirror and asking the difficult questions to find why we aren't achieving our dream sales numbers. David Stern's catchphrase: "Are You For Real ?!" is both a question and an exclamation. While working with Stern, he will help you find your authentic self—away from all career-hindering insecurities and excuses. When you're at home in your true essence, you will be in tiptop fighting form to close deals.

Evaluation Test

The Evaluation Test is the foundation for building or rebuilding your career with David Stern. It's a powerful tool that reveals the essence of the client as a salesperson—it's as if Stern is ghosting during one of your transactions. He will tailor a training regimen to you, working with you to strengthen your closing skills and make you the salesperson you want to be.

Contact David Stern today for a complimentary thirty-minute coaching session to learn what he can do to help you achieve your dreams.

www.CoachStern.com

david@coachstern.com

(917) 974-4547

BOOK
DAVID STERN
TO SPEAK

David Stern's paternal charisma, boundless love for sales, and his four decades salesperson career make his sales keynote speech a galvanizing event. His talks are like fiery and uplifting sermons eloquently making the life and career connection.

- "I believe that the bullshtick prison is about the excuses that we make that helps us stay in our own created prison."

- "When you share the value of a product you love, you don't have to sell it."

- "If you don't have goals, and, if you don't have a vision on paper for what you need to do in order to get your goals, than I'm sorry to tell you, you don't have any goals."

Contact David for a complimentary pre-speech interview to find out if he's available for your next event.

www.CoachStern.com
david@coachstern.com
(917) 974-4547